THE UNITED STATES
EARLY SILVER DOLLARS

FROM

1794 TO 1803

By M. H. BOLENDER

The assistance of Julius Reiver in the revision of this edition,
and of Aubrey Bebee in earlier editions of this book is gratefully
acknowledged by the publisher.

Fourth Revised Edition
Published by
Krause Publications, Inc.
700 E. State St.
Iola, WI 54990

ISBN: 0-87341-067-X
Library of Congress: 81-86113

Milferd H. Bolender (1894-1977)

Known as "The Dean of American Numismatics," by virtue of his long and honorable dealings with the hobby community as a dealer in coins and paper money and his work as a numismatic historian, M.H. Bolender was involved in coin collecting for 70 years. Mr. Bolender began collecting coins in Orangeville, Ill., in 1906 when his grandfather gave him a bag of 70 old coins as a reward for excellence in scholastics. Fascinated by an 1822 English gold sovereign in the group, he wrote to the Money and Stamp Brokerage Co., in New York City. His first numismatic purchase was not coins, however, but a coin book which he read and re-read until he had it memorized. His first coin purchase was a colonial New Jersey cent for which he paid 45 cents. Mr. Bolender began dealing in coins at the age of 15, selling to traveling salesmen and others who stopped at the hotels operated by his parents and grandparents in Illinois, and to schoolmates and fellow commuters on his daily 22-mile train ride to and from school. In the summer of 1910, Mr. Bolender took a job in heavy construction, working 10 hours a day for 15 cents an hour to finance purchases of rolls of the then-new 1909-S VDB Lincoln cents at $3 per roll, and rolls of 1908-S Indian cents at $1.50 a roll. After graduating from high school, Mr. Bolender served with the U.S. Infantry in World War I and upon discharge in 1919, began a 13-year career as a school teacher. It was also in 1919 that he began to send out special selling lists of coins and paper money, soon substituting regular mail bid sales. When the coin business became too big to handle on a parttime basis, Mr. Bolender left the classroom to become a full-time professional numismatist. In 57 years in the business, Mr. Bolender conducted 197 sales, and estimated that he had bought and sold over one million coins. A professional high point in his career came when he was chosen to conduct the first coin auction in conjunction with an American Numismatic Association convention, the 1929 event in Chicago. Mr. Bolender considered the climax of his career the publication of the first edition of this book in 1950. In 1960 Mr. Bolender retired from the coin dealing ranks although he maintained a personal interest in the hobby thereafter. He served as a contributor to the *Red Book* and from 1961 to early 1964 he wrote the popular column, "M.H. Bolender Writes:" for *Numismatic News,* giving readers a first-hand narrative of the hobby in the early part of the century and offering tips on coin care, numismatic investment and more. His column ended in 1964 with a second retirement from active numismatics. At the 1975 A.N.A. convention in Los Angeles, Mr. Bolender was honored with a Golden Anniversary award for 50 years membership in the national organization. He died Nov. 15, 1977, in Spring Valley, Calif., at the age of 83.

THE UNITED STATES SILVER DOLLARS
FROM 1794 TO 1803

Introduction

THE early silver dollars of the United States have long enjoyed ever increasing popularity among both new and advanced collectors in this country. It is quite natural that the *unit* of our coinage, the largest coin of any series, should be much desired by numismatists. In view of this, and considering that no less than eighty-four different obverse dies and at least seventy-five distinct reverse dies have been used during the years from 1794 to 1803 and these have been mated in various combinations or "marriages" to produce no less than one hundred fourteen separate and distinct die varieties, some kind of practical and useful book illustrated with plates should be welcomed by busy dealers and the collecting public.

The only serious attempt to prepare a thorough list of this series was made by John W. Haseltine 75 years ago, when he began a careful and vigorous study of the early silver dollars before 1804 in a very special way. Haseltine looked through all the dealers' stocks as well as most important collections of that day. This was much easier to do than it would be today. In those days, there were few dealers, and nearly all resided in Philadelphia and New York. The stocks were large but few. Today, the stocks are widely scattered among a great many dealers, and there are a hundred times as many collectors, thus spreading the supply of coins so thin that information is much more difficult to assemble. Mr. Haseltine worked thus for over five years, when, in 1881, he decided to sell his collection. His catalogue of this sale listed with his other coins, his collection of early silver dollars with his full descriptions in detail, and all the coins were sold. As stated in the original catalogue of Haseltine known as his "Type-Table Catalogue", he intended to publish a book on the subject, perhaps with plates, but with the sale of his collection, this never could materialize.

A "Descriptive List of Die Varieties of Early Silver Dollars" appeared in the Coin and Medal Bulletin in 1916. The descriptions and plates were by Wayte Raymond, but the list was not intended to be complete. We admire these arduous efforts, and Haseltine's years of work, and his thoroughness. But Haseltine's list has not been a practical and useful reference, and lacked plates. Busy dealers have refused to use it. Without any quick-finding lists, tables, or distinguishing features it took too long to attribute coins, and even then dealers were not sure of the number in many cases. Chapman, who usually described most coins well, was among the poorest to describe the early dollars; he seldom found the distinguishing features. Thomas L. Elder was one of the best cataloguers to describe the important features. Stickney, Parmelee, Earle, Atwater, and many of America's greatest collectors all collected the die varieties, but no one ever attempted to systematically catalogue them except Haseltine. And he was not pleased with his own work and intended to prepare a better book on the subject over seventy years ago!

The material for this book was gathered by me over a period of forty years! My first silver dollar, a 1795 with a hole, was acquired by me in 1906 from my grandfather, who gave me a bag of old coins, his collection, because I "made the best grades in school of the seven grandchildren". That started me collecting 44 years ago. The assembly of this collection has been difficult mainly because varieties were so often not properly described. When they were attributed according to Haseltine, the numbers were wrong very often. In one large shipment of early dollars to me, every Haseltine number was incorrect. Big dealers would not try to attribute then. "Too busy" was the reply. However, certain varieties are worth two or three times catalogue prices. At several of the annual conventions of the American Numismatic Association my collection of this series was exhibited, in New York, Philadelphia, Washington, Chicago, and other cities. For several years, dealer friends and collector specialists have pleaded with me to prepare a practical book with plates.

During the past forty years of active collecting and dealing in coins, I have examined about five thousand silver dollars before 1804, in my search for this set. Fortunately now, I kept a record of the frequency of which each variety occurs, that is, the number of each variety I have examined. Enlarging on Haseltine's efforts in his information on rarity, I have given the degree of rarity. Rarity 1 rates the most common varieties, and the degree progresses to rarity 8, where only a few are probably in existence. In some cases only one or two specimens of a variety are known to me, but I have declined to imagine that no other such coins exist.

In this book, I have kept my numbers to correspond with those of Haseltine, since his arrangement was really quite thorough, the years have proven, and the collector with numbers on their envelopes will not have to change them. It is recommended, however, that he *verify* them. For accuracy, I have been obliged to point out the few unavoidable errors in Haseltine's admirable work, and I have added the varieties since discovered. Where die cracks and minor varieties are known to me I have listed them as sub-varieties, with letters added to the numbers. The die cracks have been described, but not illustrated in the plates, since these can be readily traced from the text.

All of the coins illustrated on the plates are in the author's collection.

It is with warmest gratitude that I express my thanks to Mr. Sydney P. Noe, Chief Curator of the American Numismatic Society, New York City, for his friendly advice and encouragement; to Mr. William C. Clark, Curator of Mediæval and Modern coins of the American Numismatic Society, for valuable suggestions and his whole-hearted assistance; to Mr. DeVere Baker, photographer of the American Numismatic Society, for his careful photography and painstaking preparation and layout of the plates; and to Mr. Sawyer McA. Mosser, Editor of the American Numismatic Society of New York, for his experienced direction of the various steps in the publication of this work, and for so much of his time given in friendly and wise counsel. All have been of great assistance in this work, and their co-operation is heartily appreciated.

This work has taken much of my time and money, and I do not now wonder that others have hesitated to attempt it. However, its preparation has brought me a great deal of pleasure, and if the book proves to be helpful and useful to fellow collectors and dealers, I shall be graciously compensated.

M. H. BOLENDER

Freeport, Illinois

April 10, 1950

HISTORY OF COINAGE
OF THE EARLY SILVER DOLLARS[1]

IN September of the year 1787, Congress received from the convention which framed the constitution of the United States, the draft of that document. In accordance with a requirement therein contained, it was immediately submitted to the several states of the Union for their assent and approval. One article of the instrument provided that congress should have the power to coin money, regulate the value thereof, and of foreign coins; and another, that no state should coin money, emit bills of credit, or make anything but gold and silver coins a tender in payment of debts. The constitution was ratified by eleven states, and was finally adopted by congress on Sept. 13, 1788.

The attention of the new congress, which began its first session March 4, 1789, was quite taken up in organizing the several departments of government, and in framing laws necessary to carry out the more immediate designs of the constitution. Anticipating the action of congress in providing a currency for the country, a proposition was made by John H. Mitchell, a foreigner, to supply the United States with copper coinage "of any size and device, of pure unalloyed copper", for the sum of fourteen pence sterling, the pound. Mitchell represented that his apparatus was such as to enable him to strike the edge at the same blow with the face. This invention, however, had before been brought to the notice of the congress of the confederation by Thomas Jefferson, while he was residing in Paris. In a letter to Francis Hopkinson dated Dec. 23, 1786 he writes: "A person here has invented a method of coining the French ecu of six livres, so as to strike both faces and the edge at one stroke." [2] Jefferson suggested that in case congress should establish a mint, one of the machines used in this process, and probably the services of Mr. Drost, the inventor, might be secured. Subsequent to the date of his letter to Mr. Hopkinson he sent to John Jay specimens of this coinage, recommending very highly their perfection, and stating that from 25,000 to 30,000 pieces a day could be coined with the assistance of only two persons, the pieces of metal having been first prepared.

The propositions of Mitchell were referred to secretary of state Jefferson, who for several reasons reported on them unfavorably,

(First) Because they were supposed to be coined in a foreign country.

[1] Bibliography—American Coinage, by John H. Hickcox 1858.
[2] Jefferson's Writings, Vol. 2.

(Second) Because transportation of the coins would expose them to acts of piracy.

(Third) We would lose the opportunity of calling in and recoining the clipped money.

(Fourth) We would lose the resource of coining up our household plate, in the instant of great distress.

(Fifth) We would lose the means of preparing artists to continue the works, when the common accidents of mortality should have deprived us of those who began them.

(Sixth) The carrying on of a coinage in a foreign country, so far as the secretary knew, was without example, and general example he considered as weighty authority.

Jefferson therefore recommended that a mint when established, should be established at home. Other propositions for coining money in foreign parts, were similarly disposed of. He at once entered into a correspondence, to ascertain whether the Swiss inventor Drost could be induced to come to this country with his implements, and be employed at the United States mint, if one should be established, or at all events, to come over and "erect the proper machinery, and instruct persons how to go on with the coinage. An agreement was made, two coining mills or screws were ordered by him, but in the end he declined coming." [1]

Immediately after hearing the report of Jefferson on the proposition of Mitchell, the congress on April 15, 1790 instructed the secretary of the treasury to prepare and report a proper plan for the establishment of a national mint. To this important charge Alexander Hamilton gave full and attentive consideration, and at the next session of congress he presented an elaborate report thereon, discussing mainly the following points:

1. What ought to be the nature of the money unit of the United States?

2. What the proportions between gold and silver?

3. What the proportion and composition of alloy in each kind?

4. Whether the expense of coinage should be defrayed by the government or out of the material itself?

5. What should be the number, denominations, sizes, and devices of the various coins?

6. Whether foreign coins should be permitted to be current or not, at what rate, and for what period?

[1] Jefferson's Writings.

The resolution of the congress of the confederation, declaring the *dollar* to be the money *unit* of the United States, as well as that regulating the value of it, had never been practically carried out, so that it was difficult to say what our money unit really was. The pound was the unit of accounts, while the old Spanish "pieces of eight" with their various values, regulated our exchanges. It was on this account that it seemed most natural that the dollar, containing a specified exact amount of pure silver, should be adopted as a unit in all cases. But an objection suggested itself in the fact that the silver dollar had no standard value, while gold had a fixed price, according to its fineness, and Hamilton regarded the unit as having been hitherto virtually attached to gold rather than to silver. Hamilton therefore urged that the money unit should not be attached to either gold or silver, because this could not be done effectually without destroying the office and character of one of them as money, and reducing it to the situation of mere merchandise. Indeed, it was his idea that if either was preferred, it ought to be gold rather than silver. His conclusions were, that the unit might correspond with 24¾ grains of pure gold, and with 371¼ grains of pure silver, each answering to a dollar in the money of accounts. The alloy in each case was to be one-twelfth of the total weight, which would make the unit 27 grains of standard gold, and 405 grains of standard silver. Each of these, it has been remarked, would answer to a dollar in the money of account. Applying to this the decimal subdivision as established Aug. 8, 1786, the unit in the money of account would continue to be a dollar, and its multiples, and dimes, cents, and mills.

Therefore Hamilton proposed the following coins:

1. A gold piece, or eagle, equal in value and weight to ten units or dollars.

2. A gold piece (dollar) equal to a tenth of the former, which shall be a unit or dollar.

3. A silver piece, which shall also be a *unit* or *dollar*.

4. A silver piece (dime) which shall be in weight and value a tenth part of the silver unit or dollar.

5. A copper piece (cent) which shall be of the value of the hundredth part of a dollar.

6. A copper piece which shall be half the value of the former.

It is not at all improbable that individuals who had implements of coinage experimented on some of the above named suggestions, in advance of any action at the mint.

Hamilton's report was transmitted to congress on Jan. 28, 1791. A concurrent resolution of the senate and house of representatives, passed March 3 of the same year, declared that a mint should be established, and that the president should cause to be engaged such principal artists as necessary to carry out the resolutions, and also to procure such apparatus as should be requisite for the same purpose.

The law "establishing the mint and regulating the coins of the United States" received the president's approval on April 2, 1792. The principal points of the coinage law included the following:

1. The officers to be employed included a director, an assayer, a chief coiner, an engraver, and a treasurer.

2. The coins to be struck were to be: Gold eagles or ten dollars, gold half-eagles or five-dollar pieces, gold quarter-eagles, *silver dollars or units,* silver half-dollars, silver quarter dollars, silver *dismes* and *half-dismes,* copper cents and half-cents.

3. The devices and legends to be stamped on the coins were to include upon one side "an impression emblematical of Liberty, with an inscription of the word LIBERTY, and the year of coinage." The reverse of the gold and silver coins should have a "figure or representation of an eagle, with the inscription UNITED STATES OF AMERICA." Upon the reverse of the copper coins, an inscription should express the denomination of the piece.

Under this coinage act of 1792 "the *silver dollars or units* were each to be of the value of the Spanish milled dollar as the same is now current, and to contain $371\frac{1}{4}$ grains of pure silver, or 416 grains of standard silver." The alloy was 179 parts to 1485 parts of fine silver.

President Washington proceeded at once to carry out the intentions of the act, and as Philadelphia was then the seat of the government, he there caused the necessary buildings and machinery to be provided and put into condition for the purpose of coining. In the autumn of the same year 1792 he informed congress that a small beginning had been made in the coinage of half-dollars and cents. Washington manifested a lively interest in the progress of this work, and frequently visited the mint. It was at this time that he brought to the mint silver bullion to be coined into half-dismes and dismes, not for currency, but intended as presents for friends.

The offices of artists, chief coiner, and assayer, were of course, considered of great importance, and it was the intention to employ those who were most skilled in these professions. As these arts had been but little practiced in our country, efforts were made to procure artisans from abroad. Jefferson again endeavored to secure the services of Drost, but not being successful, Mr. Pinckney, who was then our minister to England, engaged Albion Coxe as assayer. Henry Voight, an artist of the United States, performed the duties of the office of chief coiner, and for a considerable length of time he also made the dies. Silver dollars were first coined in the latter part of 1794.

Many difficulties, however, attended the early minting operations. The establishment was more extensive than any which had heretofore been erected in this country, and experiments had to be made at almost every step in its progress. Workmen who had been engaged in Europe often failed to come, and others were not masters of their business. Materials for the machinery were with difficulty procured, even the tools necessary to make the machinery and implements were first to be made, and both were manufactured at the mint. These were prepared chiefly under the direction of Mr. Voight. The construction of the mint was mainly upon theory, which of course, created greater delay and expense than full practical knowledge would have found necessary. The cost of building, apparatus, and machinery up to February 1795 was $22,720. This was a large sum in those days. Up to that date there were three presses, one of which could coin 10,000 cents in a day. The machinery was moved by horse power.

The public was disappointed in the lack of economy in mint operations. The people also expected greater relief from the hardships of diminished copper circulation in the country. The expense of the mint was considerable for operations, and increased from year to year. An opinion generally prevailed that the establishment was unnecessarily expensive and in fact "less productive than was rationally expected by its friends and advocates." There was some foundation for this complaint. One of the principles of the act establishing the mint was, that the whole coinage, including refining, was to be executed at the public expense, the depositor being fully indemnified. Thus, the person who brought bullion in the debased state to the mint, received in return as much coin for the standard metal contained therein, as he whose bullion had been previously refined, so that the expense of assaying and refining was a public charge. Again, the mint had no means of purchasing bullion. Every deposit of metal had to be coined as soon as possible, in order that the depositor might not lose the benefit of the use of the coin. Therefore the clippings and grains of each deposit were necessarily on each occasion of deposit, melted. With the means on hand of payment at once of the amount due on deposits, the coinage of such deposits might have been more conveniently and more economically carried on. The small deposits would then have been kept in vaults until a large amount had been accumulated, and then coined, as the expense of coining a small quantity of bullion was nearly as great as that of an amount many times larger.

Leading men of the country began to doubt the propriety of continuing a government establishment which, as they contended, cost more than the benefits derived from it. There was an opinion that the Bank of the United States could coin for the nation at a less expense, or that the work could be done by contract. Propositions had already been made to the secretary of the treasury, to undertake to supply the coins of the United States, in case the mint should be abolished.

In January of 1802 the house of representatives voted to repeal the coinage acts of 1791, but the senate voted "No" and upheld the coinage act, and the establishment of the mint. In the autumn of the same year, it was again considered and debated. It was known that the senate was still opposed to repeal. Many considered the mint and equipment too inadequate to continue. The property was indeed meagre. The lots were too small, the machinery and horses were worn out, and perhaps it would be necessary to provide steam power.

In these early days the mint property consisted of two lots on 7th street between Market and Arch streets, with a dwelling house on the north lot, and a shell of a house and a stable on the south lot. There was also a lot on Sugar Alley, and a frame building improved for a large furnace, in the commons at the north end of 6th Street. There were three horses, good for little but for the use in the mint. The director of the mint thought that the horses might last another year.

Other equipment included about 22 tons of copper planchets, five coining presses with machinery, three cutting presses, one milling machine, five pairs of rollers, one drawing machine. Other things listed in an old report included three pair of smith's bellows, a set of blacksmith tools, carpenter's tools, seven stoves, one turning lathe, and a large number of hubs and dies. There were six scale beams, scales and weights, two sets of assay scales, and sundry adjusting scales, as well as the engraver's tools, pots, bottles, and an old horse, cart, and gears. Furniture in the clerk's room was listed, also 2000 bushels of charcoal and about 2000 fire brick.

Considering this condition of affairs, the house of representatives adopted a resolution directing inquiry as to the amount the whole property of the mint would probably sell for, and the expense of more suitable buildings, machinery, etc.

However, at the same session of congress, a law was passed continuing the coinage act of 1792 for five years, which was repeatedly renewed every five years until 1828, when it was enacted, that the act of March 3, 1801 should remain in force and operation until otherwise provided by law. Thus, the early days in the mint presented many problems.

HINTS FOR STUDY

COLLECTORS are urged to read the general paragraphs for the coinage of each year they desire to study. The tables and quick-finding lists are a practical help to attribute coins in the shortest time. When a number is tentatively found, it is well to check same with the detailed description for that number, and with the plate.

A study of the die cracks, breaks, defects, and failures in the dies has been given for the benefit of the advanced collector whose fancy prompts him to secure more than one specimen of a number. This list is not expected to be complete, and it is hoped that collectors will enjoy the thrill of the discovery of new varieties, or die breaks. Such possibilities always will continue to exist.

The edge or rim of every early silver dollar included in this work reads HUNDRED CENTS ONE DOLLAR OR UNIT. The weight was established by law to be 416 grains, and the fineness 892.4.

1794

Only one pair of dies was used in striking the silver dollars in 1794. Only 1758 pieces were coined. Usually found with the impression weak on lower part of date and the stars on left, and sometimes the border milling on left does not show up. The corresponding portion of reverse, especially the word STATES, will therefore also appear weak. Very rare.

OBVERSE First star close to 1 in date. Second star near curl, but does not touch it. No head of 1795 is exactly like this head.

REVERSE 21 leaves on each branch. Wreath has 19 berries, 10 on left branch, 9 on right. A leaf is joined to second T in STATES. Eagle's wing touches R in AMERICA. This die was not used in 1795.

Copper trial or experimental pieces of 1794 were struck from the above dies, one before the stars were punched into the die. At least one piece in copper is known without the stars, and at least one in copper with the stars. The author has seen a piece with stars in copper, silver-plated.

1795

All of the silver dollars of this year, as well as those of 1794 and 1796 have fifteen stars. 11 different obverse dies and 12 reverse dies were used in various combinations to strike twenty distinct varieties. There are 18 varieties of flowing hair type, and 2 varieties of the fillet bust type, which was adopted during the year and continued the following years. 184,013 pieces of all varieties were struck in 1795.

There is no exact head of 1794. For many years dealers have listed 1795 variety with "head of 1794". Strictly speaking there is no such coin. None of the heads of 1795 closely resemble the head of 1794. My numbers 1 and 3 *most nearly resemble* the head of 1794, and my number 7 is most often sold as "head of 1794". See notes under those numbers.

1795 SILVER DOLLARS

Bolender No.	Haseltine No.	Obverse Die used for	Reverse Die used for	Berries L-R	Leaves	Rarity	Remarks
1	1	1-10-16	1-2-13	9-10	2	3	Wide date spaced 1 795. 5 prominent curls, and another thin curl below 3rd curl from top.
2	2	2-17-19	1-2-13	9-10	2	2	Diagonal bar in field close to inner point of 4th star. Close 95.
3	3	3-9-11	3	8-8	2	4	Only variety with 16 berries, 8 on each branch.
4	4	4	4-9	9-8	2	4	Last star entirely under bust.
5	5	5	5-6-12	7-6	3	1	Diagonal bar in field close to uppermost curl extending toward inner point of 5th star.
6	6	6	5-6-12	7-6	3	3	6 curls, not touching star. Three leaves.
7	7	7-18-20	7-19	7-7	3	4	One of two varieties with 14 berries, 7 on each branch.
8	8	8	8-20	9-10	2	7	High bust, close to LIBERTY.
9	9	3-9-11	4-9	9-8	2	5	Obv. B-3, rev. B-4.
10	10	1-10-16	10-17	9-9	2	6	2 berries on outside of wreath on right, between eagle's wing and ribbon.
11	11	3-9-11	11	9-10	2	7	Check berry arrangement in description.
12	12	12	5-6-12	7-6	3	6	Curl passes through star 13-berry reverse.
12-A	—	12-A	12-A	7-6	3	7	Die break through 7 to bust.
13	13	13	1-2-13	9-10	2	6	Wide date, 79 closest. 19 berries.
14	14	14	14	7-	—	3	Fillet bust, not well-centered.
15	15	15	15	6-	—	4	Fillet bust well-centered.
16	New	1-10-16	16	9-10	2	7	Flowing hair. 19 berries. Reverse: point of 3rd leaf on right outside of wreath under center of I in AMERICA.
17	New	2-17-19	10-17	10-9	2	7	Flowing hair. Obv. B-2. 19 berries. Rev. B-10.
18	New	7-18-20	18	8-11	2	7	Flowing hair. No outer berry under A in STATES. Specimen known in Eliasberg collection.
19	New	2-17-19	7-19	7-7	3	6	Diagonal bar in field close to inner point of 4th star. Close 95. One of only 2 varieties with 14 berries.
20	New	7-18-20	8-20	9-10	2	7	Obv. B-7, Rev. B-8.

[14]

1795. B-1 (H-1)

OBVERSE — Flowing hair in five prominent curls, *with a thin faint curl addi tional* below the third curl from the top. One point of lowest star on left just touches lowest curl. The curl continues upward to half close the loop. This same obverse die was used for B-10 and B-16. The date is wide, with more space between 1 and 7 than other figures. This obverse resembles the head of 1794, as the nose and mouth, and top of head are similar, but the lowest curl is much thicker on the 1794. None of the 1795 dollars have the exact head of 1794.

REVERSE — Two leaves under each wing of eagle. A leaf ends directly below center of first S in STATES and another leaf ends just under left corner of upright of E in STATES. The wreath is delicate, leaves small, berries large. Two berries opposite I in UNITED and two opposite I in AMERICA, on both inside and outside of wreath. One of these large berries is below *right* corner of I in UNITED, another below left corner of I in AMERICA. Same reverse die used for B-2 and B-13. A common variety.

1795. B-2 (H-2)

OBVERSE — Flowing hair in six prominent curls. The lowest curl is pierced and separated by a point of first star, and the curl is continued upwards to almost close its loop. Wide date, the 95 closer together than the other figures. The upper left star is 2 mm. distant from L in LIBERTY, and is farther from the L than in any other variety. A diagonal "bar" slightly more than 1½ mm. long appears in the left field close to inner point of 4th star, this bar extending diagonally northwest to southeast. This obverse die was also used for B-17 and B-19.

REVERSE — From same die as B-1, the die was also used for B-13.

1795. B-3 (H-3)

OBVERSE — Flowing hair in six curls; the third one from the top *turns downward and touches* the fourth curl. Two points of first star touch the lowest curl which ends at star point. The last star or lowest one on the right is mostly under the bust, and a point nearly touches. Close date; outlines appear at top of 5 and right top of 7. Often called the "head of 1794" because of two low thick curls. This obverse die was also used for B-9 and B-11.

REVERSE *The only variety with 16 berries,* 8 on each branch of wreath. There are only *two berries* on left branch, between eagle's wing and ribbon bow, both on inside of wreath. Two leaves under each wing. Scarce. Rarity 4.

1795. B-4 (H-4)

OBVERSE Flowing hair in six curls; lowest curl ends faintly above two points of first star, and close to one point. Close date, figures 9 and 5 closest, and the distance between the 1 and 7 about the same as between the first star and figure 1. Star closer to date than in any other variety, about 1½ mm. *The 15th or last star is entirely under the bust.* The 14th star has a point near bust. Small lump under chin. Die flaws appear close to border near 10th and 11th stars.

REVERSE *17 berries,* 9 on left branch, 8 on right. A berry on outside of wreath midway between S and T of STATES, the only variety in which this occurs. Same reverse die was used for B-9. Scarce. Rarity 4.

1795. B-5 (H-5)

OBVERSE Flowing hair in six curls, the third and fourth close together. Lowest curl distant from star. A "bar" over 2 mm. long extends diagonally from close to top curl toward point of 5th star. Look for the *"bar" near uppermost curl.* (B-2 has the bar near 4th star.) Wide date, the 1 and 7 farthest apart. First star about as close to 1 as 7 is to 9.

REVERSE *13 berries,* 7 on left branch, 6 on right. Three leaves under each wing of eagle. Two berries under first T in STATES, one on inside and one on outside of wreath. This die was also used for B-6 and B-12. All specimens of B-5 and B-6 examined by me show a fine die crack from end of left stem downward, in B-5 extending to border. However, the crack does not appear in B-12 nor B-12a. This is by far the most common variety of 1795. Rarity 1.

1795. B-6

This is a new discovery, unknown to Hazeltine and Bolender.

OBVERSE
Same die as used for B-13. Foot of R is short, having been made with a broken punch. E is punched over an R. Lowest curl barely misses a point of the first star, but continues on to touch and slightly pass a second point of the same star.

REVERSE
Same die as used for B-5 and B-12, except that the cluster of leaves under the first S in STATES contains only 3 leaves. Rarity 7.

1795. B-6a (Original B-6) (H-6)

OBVERSE
The die has been lapped, shortening all of the curls. The lowest curl now ends between two points of the first star. The foot of R has been lengthened with an engraving tool, and now has an awkward, irregular appearance. The R under E is very weak, but can still be seen.

REVERSE
A fourth leaf has been added to the cluster under the first S in STATES. Rarity 3.

1795. B-7 (H-7)

OBVERSE
Flowing hair in six curls. The lowest curl is very small and perfect, and touches a point of first star, as it continues to nearly complete a loop. Last star partly under bust, but not as far under as B-3, and not quite as close, but it is near. (Note.—In B-4 the last star is *entirely* under bust.) Wide date, most space between 1 and 7. Same die as B-18, B-20.

REVERSE
The only 14-berry variety. Seven berries on each branch. There is *only one* berry on left branch of wreath between eagle's wing and ribbon bow, and it is on the inside of wreath. Three leaves under each wing. Same die as B-19.

This variety has also sometimes been listed as "head of 1794", but there is no exact head of 1794. Rarity 4.

[17]

1795. B-8 (H-8)

OBVERSE   Flowing hair in six curls; the bottom curl is slender and long, touching a point of first star and curling upwards. The second curl from the bottom points downward to a point of second star. Last star is farther from the 5 in date than in any other variety, about 4½ mm. Wide date. The *head is not well-centered,* but too high and too far to left. Head is close to LIBERTY.

REVERSE   A berry on outside of wreath slightly left of left stand of first A in AMERICA, and another berry on inside of wreath opposite second stand of same letter, distinguishes this 19-berry reverse from all others. Two leaves under each wing. Same die as B-20.

In 40 years the author has seen only two specimens! One of these was handled by him four times, but was recognized as the same example. Doubtless a very few others are hidden away in collections, but without any doubts, B-8 is "excessively rare" as stated by Haseltine. His specimen was not in the Haseltine sale catalogue of 1881, having been withdrawn beforehand and sold privately. Rarity 7.

1795. B-9 (H-9)

OBVERSE   From the same die as B-3 and B-11.

REVERSE   From the same die as B-4. Very rare. Rarity 5.

1795. B-10 (H-10)

OBVERSE   From the same die as B-1 and B-16.

REVERSE   19 berries, *nine on left branch* and 9 on right. A berry on outside of wreath opposite C in AMERICA, *and* only one berry opposite last A in AMERICA, that being on inside of wreath. *Two berries on outside of wreath on right between eagle's wing and ribbon bow.* Same die used for B-17. Extremely rare. Rarity 6.

1795. B-11 (H-11)

OBVERSE From the same die as B-3 and B-9.

REVERSE 19 berries, 9 on left branch, 10 on right. *Differs from any other 19-berry reverse,* as follows:—Two berries in wreath under A in STATES, the one on inside of wreath under center of A, and the one on outside of wreath under left corner of right foot of A. Only one berry in wreath under OF, and it is on the inside of wreath. Two berries, one inside of wreath, and one outside, are close together under first S in STATES, and two more close together under first A in AMERICA. Two leaves under each wing.

Haseltine's specimen was only good, and scratched in field, the only one he could find. A specimen listed in an important sale a few years ago as H-11 was purchased by me, but turned out to be H-2, and there was no H-11 in the sale. I have found but one example. Excessively rare. Rarity 7.

1795. B-12 (H-12)

OBVERSE Flowing hair in six curls, the *lowest curl passing through a point of first star,* and continues to right, ending in a sharp point. Second curl from bottom points downward to space between two points of second star. Wide date, the 7 and 9 closer than other figures. Letters IB spaced too widely. Letter B leans to right, as do also the T and Y.

REVERSE 13 berries. From same die as B-5 and B-6. Three leaves under each wing. Rarity 6.

1795. B-12a

Same as B-12, but variety with vertical die break extending from bust to border through 7 of date. The author's specimen was formerly in the great Stickney collection lot No. 807 in the Stickney sale held by Henry Chapman in 1907. Mr. Chapman there described the die break. No other specimen has been found by the author. Rarity 7.

1795. B-13 (H-13)

OBVERSE   From the same die as B-6. Flowing hair in six curls; lowest curl barely misses a point of first star, but continues on to touch and slightly pass a second point of same star. THe second curl from bottom turns downward pointing to space between two points of second star. *Wide date, 79 closest.*

REVERSE   19 berries.   From same die as B-1 and B-2.

Haseltine had met with only a single specimen, and called it "probably unique".   This number was noticeably missing in that great sale of the "World's greatest collection" held by the Numismatic Gallery in January, 1945.   The author's example is probably the Haseltine specimen.   Two others are known to the author, and no others have been heard of in 40 years.   Rarity 7.

1795. B-14 (H-14)

OBVERSE   Fillet bust, the hair tied up in a ribbon at back.   *The bust was not properly centered* in the die work, being placed too far to the left.

REVERSE   Small eagle, considerably smaller than on any of the preceding varieties.   Eagle stands on clouds.   Wreath is composed of a palm branch (right) and olive branch (left), the latter with seven berries.   Rarity 3.

1795. B-15 (H-15)

OBVERSE   Draped fillet bust similar to last, but the *bust is well-centered* in the die work.

REVERSE   Similar to B-14, but only 6 berries in olive branch.   Rarity 4.

1795. B-16 (Reverse new)

OBVERSE   From the same die as B-1 and B-10.

REVERSE   19 berries, nine on left branch, ten on right. A berry on outside of wreath only, opposite first stand of N in UNITED, and a berry on outside of wreath opposite center of first A in AMERI-CA. A berry on inside of wreath opposite center of M. *No berry* opposite either I on outside of wreath. *Point of third leaf on right outside of wreath under center* of I in AMERICA.

Unknown to Haseltine, the author's example is a proof, and the only specimen he has seen or heard of in forty years' collecting. Rarity 8.

1795. B-17 (New)

OBVERSE   From same die as B-2, B-19.

REVERSE   From same die as B-10.

This coin has not been seen or heard of by any present day collectors. No other example has turned up. Possibly the Clark coin was misattributed, and this vareity does not exist.

This combination is excessively rare. Not known to Haseltine. The only specimen known to the author was in the famous Primus C. Clark collection, catalogued and sold by Mr. Bolender in 1932. Rarity 8.

1795. B-18 (New)

OBVERSE   From same die as B-7, B-20.

REVERSE   Only reverse die with 8 berries on left, 11 on right. No outer berry under A in STATES. Unknown to Haseltine or Bolender. Specimen known in Eliasberg Collection.

1795. B-19 (New)

OBVERSE   From same die as B-2, B-17.

REVERSE   From same die as B-7.

Specimen reported in the Frank Stirling Collection.

1795. B-20 (New)

OBVERSE   From same die as B-7, B-18.

REVERSE   From same die as B-8.

Specimen reported in the Frank Stirling Collection.

THE SILVER DOLLARS OF 1796

(Total Coinage 72,920)

1796. B-1 (H-1)

OBVERSE — *Small date,* the 9 and 6 closer together than other figures. *Two points* of star touch curl. 15 stars, as all have, of this year.

REVERSE — *Small letters* in legend, 7 berries in wreath. *None of the leaves* touch legend. Small eagle on clouds.

NOTE. This identical reverse die was used, always sparingly for small coinages, with six different obverses, *over a period of four years!* This reverse die was used for 1795 B14; 1796 B-1, B-2, B-3; 1797 B-2 the rare small letter 1797; 1798 B-2 the rare 15-star variety with small eagle.

1796. B-2 (H-2)

OBVERSE — *Small wide date;* all of the figures of date *evenly spaced* wide apart. Curl touches *only one point of first star.*

REVERSE — Small letters. From same die as 1795 B-14; 1796 B-1 and B-3; 1797 B-2, and 1798 B-2. Scarce.

1796. B-3 (H-3)

OBVERSE — *Small wide date,* the 9 and 6 closer together than other figures, the

Most experts now question whether this variety actually exists.

top of 6 tipped more to left. The 9 is a trifle high with its top tipped too much to the right. Lowest *star on left does not quite touch hair.* Die flaw like "tear-drop" beneath 11th star, and several beneath 13th star. Die dot above 1 of date. The stars are small and a number of them on the right imperfect. Curl on top of the head defective. The letters in LIBERTY are not bifurcated.

NOTE. This is the same obverse die as used for B-4, except for die corrections as described under that number. It is identical with B-4a listed below.

REVERSE — Small letters. From same die as 1795 B-14; 1796 B-1 and B-2; 1797 B-2, and 1798 B-2. Die touched up, some letters now appear bifurcated.

While many 1796 dollars have been listed as H-3, this has been erroneously done. I have purchased a dozen or more H-3's, every one of them wrongly attributed. Only three specimens are known to me.

[22]

1796.   B-4 (H-4)

OBVERSE From same obverse die as B-3, with the following corrections by the engraver.   The curl on top of head and stars on right are perfect.   The letters in LIBERTY are bifurcated.

REVERSE *Large letters* in legend.   Most letters bifurcated.   Eight plain berries in wreath.

1796.   B-4a

OBVERSE From same die as B-3, and showing the same die imperfections as that number.   Curl on top of head defective.   LIBERTY not bifurcated.

REVERSE From same die as B-4.   Large letters, which are not bifurcated. Extremely rare.   The only specimen I have found.   From the John T. Reeder collection.   Mr. Reeder purchased it from Henry Chapman's sale of the Gable collection.

1796.   B-5 (H-5)

OBVERSE *Large date.*   The 6 in date plainly shows it was double-cut at top.

REVERSE *Small letters.*   Seven large berries in wreath, and a very small 8th berry is made to show on inside stem of lowest sprig of leaves on left.   Wreath differs from any other variety, *several* LEAVES *touching letters* of legend.   Die lump at right top of I in AMERICA *does not touch* C.

1796.   B-5a

From same dies as B-5, but the die lump is now larger, and extends well along letter C.

Another specimen of this variety is a curious overstrike.   The reverse is struck over the obverse of this variety, the date and stars showing plainly on the reverse.

1796 B-6. (New)

OBVERSE From same die as B-2.

REVERSE Large letters. Lowest outer berry is between N and I in UNITED. 4 berries inside the wreath, 4 berries outside. Heavy vertical die break from rim to rim touching left side of O, and running through the center of C. This is an interesting break, because the 20% of the coin to the right of it is strongly struck, and appears to be at least two grades higher in condition than the rest of the coin, which is weakly struck.

THE 1797 SILVER DOLLARS

In 1797 the number of stars was increased to sixteen. The coinage was the smallest of any year from 1795 to 1803, only 7776 pieces having been struck. Only two obverse dies and three reverse dies were required for this small coinage.

1797. B-1 (H-1)

OBVERSE   16 stars, seven on right facing bust.

REVERSE   Large letters in legend. 8 berries in left branch. Lowest berry near ribbon bow is on *inside* of wreath.

1797. B-1a

Same as B-1 but with die cracks through 97 of date, bust, and stars on right. Another crack from upper back curl through ribbon and seventh star.

1797. B-1b

OBVERSE   Same as B-1a, but the cracks are now more pronounced. Additional cracks appear from lower border upward through 9 of date, bust, and curls through second star to border. Others appear in parallel waves from top curls on head to letters ERTY.

REVERSE   Die now shows a crack from border through top of TE in STATES. Another crack from border down through second T in STATES to wreath.

1797. B-1c

Same as B-1b, but advanced stages of the die breaks, with numerous additional cracks, 9th star down to ribbon, neck through chin, right field to 12th star, and others.

1797. B-2 (H-2)

OBVERSE   From same die as B-1.

REVERSE   *Small letters.* From same die as 1795 B-14; 1796 B-1, B-2, and B-3; and 1798 B-2.   Very rare.

1797. B-3 (H-3)

OBVERSE   16 stars, *only six at right* facing bust.

REVERSE   Large letters in legend.   8 berries in left branch.   Lowest berry near ribbon bow is on *outside* of wreath.

LIBERTY and some other letters bifurcated.   Large planchet.

1797. B-3a

Same as B-3, but none of the letters are bifurcated, and the planchet is considerably smaller.

THE SILVER DOLLARS OF 1798

THE year 1798 brought about the transition to the 13 stars on the dollar, and they appear for the first time, although one number (B-2) retains the 15 stars. When a die cracked it was often still used for coinage. Since the author collected die breaks as well as die varieties, and since these die cracks help to more easily attribute some die varieties, it was thought best to list those in the writer's collection. Plates of these have been omitted. Spurs on the 9 show plainly on numbers 10, 12, 13, 14, 15, 22, 23, and 25. All from B-1 to B-7 have the knobbed 9 in date, and all from B-8 to B-31 are without the knob to the 9. Use the tables to save time, and then verify with the description and the plates.

The total coinage for the year was 327,536 pieces, coined from 19 obverse and 20 reverse dies combined to make 31 major die varieties. The notes on rarity are based on the author's records of frequency over a period of forty years, and only on specimens actually examined by him.

1798 DOLLARS OBVERSE

OBVERSE	BERRIES ON REVERSE						*POSITION OF LEAF					EAGLE'S BEAK			
	5 Small 2 Above Close	5 Medium 2 Above Close	5—Three Above Equidistant	5 Large—2nd & 3rd From Top Close	5 Very Small	4 Only	Under Space Between R & I	Under Left Point of I	Under Left Upright of I	Under Center of I	Slightly Right of Center of I	Star Distant	Star Close Or Near	Star Touches Upper Part	Star Touches Lower Part
Knob on 9 (Nos. 1 to 7 and 32)	6	4, 32	3, 5, 7				3, 7	4, 32	5, 6			3, 7	6	4, 5, 32	
17 close	12										12				12
Medium wide date	10-11, 13-14, 24						11	13, 14	10, 24			10-11, 13		14, 24	
Wide date	15, 16						15, 16					15, 16			
Very wide date	19	18, 21	20				20	18, 19, 21				18-19, 20-21			
Very wide date 8 touching bust	22, 23			17				22, 23	17			22, 23	17		
Close date	25			9		8			8, 25, 33			9	8	25	
Close date with high 8	26, 27, 29, 30, 31, 33	28					27, 30			26, 31	28, 29	27, 28	31, 33	26, 30	29

* Under I in America.
No. 9—Point of leaf under right point of R in AMERICA.

Quick Finding List

1798 SILVER DOLLARS

Number		*Arrows*
1	Knob 9. Thirteen stars. Small eagle.	
2	Knob 9. Fifteen stars. Small eagle.	
3	Knob. 9. Curl does not touch 1. Rx. large eagle. Star distant from eagle's beak.	13
4	Knob 9. Curl does not touch 1. Leaf under left point of I in AMERICA.	10 perfect, 1 faint, & 2 sticks
5	Knob. 9. Curl does not touch 1. Large eagle.	10 + 3 heads without sticks
6	Knob 9. Curl touches 1. Rx. star near beak, but does not touch. 5 small berries, the two upper ones closest together.	10 + 2 sticks
7	Knob 9. Curl touches 1. Rx. star distant from eagle's beak.	13
8	Close date. Only 4 large berries.	13
9	Close date. Rx. 5 large berries, second and third from top are closest together.	12
10	Medium wide date. Spur on 9. Die flaw between last star and bust.	13
11	Medium wide date. No spur on 9. Hill-shaped die-cutting shows just beneath ribbon bow along two highest curls at back of head.	13
12	In date, 17 close together. Rx. star touches lower part of eagle's beak.	13
13	Medium wide date. Die "flaw" between last star & bust.	10
14	Medium wide date. Spur on 9. Lines in field between curl and first star.	13
15	Wide date, spur on 9. Rx. leaf points to space between R and I in AMERICA.	13
16	Wide date, spur on 9. Letters in LIBE are close together, ERTY wider apart. Die break top 179 to left border.	13
17	Very wide date, 8 just touching bust. Rx. with 5 very small berries.	10
18	Very wide date, 8 near bust, but not touching. Die lump between date and bust. Leaf under left point of I in AMERICA.	13
19	Very wide date, distant from bust.	13
20	Very wide date, 1 close to curl. Die lump between date and bust. Leaf points between R and I in AMERICA.	13
21	Very wide date, 1 close to curl. Die lump between date and bust.	10 arrows and a "stick"

Number		Arrows
22	Very wide date, 8 firmly united with bust. Rx. die break down through E of STATES.	13
23	Very wide date, 8 firmly united with bust. Die flaw on reverse above third upper star from right.	13
24	Medium wide date. Rx. star touches upper part of eagle's beak.	13
25	Close date, "whisker" on chin. Rx. star touches upper part of eagle's beak.	13
26	Close date, high 8. Rx. star touches upper part of eagle's beak.	12 arrows and a "stick"
27	Close date, high 8. Rx. leaf under space between R and I. Star distant from eagle's beak.	13
28	Close date, high 8. Rx. leaf slightly right of center of I. Star distant from eagle's beak.	13
29	Close date, high 8. Rx. star touches lower part of eagle's beak.	13
30	Close date, high 8. Rx. stars all distant from clouds. Leaf points under space between I and R. Star touches upper part of eagle's beak.	13
31	Close date, high 8. Rx. leaf points under center of I in AMERICA. Star close to both points of eagle's beak, but does not touch.	13
32	Knob 9. Right side of curl near leaf under left point of I in AMERICA.	1 Missing, 10 Perfect, 1 Faint, & 2 sticks
33	Close date, high 8. Star almost touches upper part of eagle's beak. No stars touch clouds. Heavy die break across reverse through right side of T in UNITED — Ealge's breast — extreme left side of M in AMERICA.	13

1798. B-1 (H-1)

OBVERSE   *13 stars.* Close date, knob 9, figures 98 close.

REVERSE   *Small eagle. Large letters.* From same reverse die as 1797 B-1b.

This variety is rare and also in good demand for type sets. Rarity 4.

1798. B-1a

Same as above but in addition to the die break on reverse down through second T in STATES and another crack through TES, there is another break from border above last S in STATES through top of OF and center of AMERIC. From same reverse die as 1797 B-1c. Very rare. Rarity 5.

1798. B-2 (H-2)

OBVERSE   *15 stars.* The only 1798 dollar with fifteen stars!

REVERSE   *Small eagle* on clouds. *Small letters* in legend. From the same reverse die as 1795 B-14; 1796 B-1, B-2, and B-3; and 1797 B-2. This identical die was used for four years, but always sparingly for small issues. Very rare. Rarity 5.

1798. B-3 (H-3)

OBVERSE   Knob 9. Thirteen stars, as are all the following. Upper left star near L, but upper right star is over 1½ mm. distant from Y. The 1 in date is near curl but does not touch it. Two die "dots" appear under E in LIBERTY, and two more on bust just above drapery, showing on all fine specimens. Same obverse die used for B-4 and B-5.

REVERSE   Large heraldic eagle, as adopted for all the following. Star distant from eagle's beak. Three stars on left between eagle's beak and clouds form a triangle. Leaf points to space between I and R in AMERICA. Stem of branch curves *outward*. Same reverse die used for B-7 and B-20. Rarity 4.

1798. B-4 (H-4)

OBVERSE   From same die as B-3.

REVERSE   Large eagle.   Upper part of eagle's beak shuts down on point of star.   Three stars on left between eagle's beak and clouds are more in a line than in form of a triangle.   Leaf points close to left corner of I in AMERICA, and 4th outside leaf tip is under right base of R in AMERICA.   Only 10 perfect arrows, 1 faint arrow, and 2 "sticks".   Extremely rare.   Rarity 6.

1798.   B-5 (H-5)

OBVERSE   From same die as B-3 and B-4.   The top of the 1 in date is straight as in my B-4, and letters in LIBERTY are bifurcated in this variety.

REVERSE   Large eagle.   Star just about touches outside of point of upper part of eagle's beak.   Top of F in OF and E in AMERICA are defective.   Only 10 arrows, and three heads additional without sticks.   A heavy vertical die break along right side of shield entirely across reverse.   Haseltine had found but a single specimen (fair), and I have seen but one.   Excessively rare.   Rarity 7.

1798.   B-6 (H-6)

OBVERSE   Knob 9.   Thirteen stars.   Point of 1 touches curl.   The 8 very nearly touches bust.   Upper right star is closer to Y than upper left star is to L.   Same obverse die used for B-7.

REVERSE   Large eagle.   Point of star is near center of space between two parts of eagle's beak, but does not touch.   Leaf points to center of I in AMERICA.   Only 10 perfect arrows, and two sticks. Die flaw about like a comma after date.   Light die crack from hair ribbon through first star thence under 1 of date, upward through 79.   The stars on right are thinner than those on left, on the obverse.   Rarity 3.

1798.   B-6a

A subvariety, B-6b, exists with Obv. of B-6, Rev. of B-17.   Same as B-6, but the die break is now heavier and more advanced. A crack has developed on reverse through the arrows and N. Rarity 5.

1798.   B-7 (H-7)

OBVERSE   From same die as B-6, without die crack.

[31]

REVERSE From same die as B-3, and B-20.

This combination is extremely rare, and I have found but two specimens. Rarity 6.

NOTE. None of the following 1798 dollars have the knob to 9 of date. All of the above have the knob.

1798. B-8 (H-8)

OBVERSE Stars on right very close to Y and bust. Long vertical die flaw in center of left obverse field. Die "dot" near edge between two denticles above left part of T in LIBERTY. A break from lower right part of E to hair.

REVERSE *Only 4 berries,* and these are large. The only 4-berry reverse of the year! Light crack from border through upper left part of E in STATES. Point of leaf under left upright of I in AMERICA. A very common variety. Rarity 1.

1798. B-8a

From same dies as B-8, but with die breaks as follows: Die crack on obverse through L to ribbon. The reverse die is now shattered with numerous breaks. A crack through top of UNIT down through ED, top of S, above TA, top of TES. Breaks through both top and bottom of OF, continue to AM, and top of ER. Another break down through C and branch to shield. Another break through arrow butts, eagle's tail, and stem to right. Very rare. Rarity 5.

1798. B-9 (H-9)

OBVERSE Compact date, 8 close to bust, being a little nearer than 1 is to curl. Upper left star close to L and lowest right star very close to bust. None of the letters in LIBERTY are bifurcated.

REVERSE Star distant from eagle's beak. 5 small berries, the second and third from top are closest together. Leaf points to lower right point of R in AMERICA. 12 arrows. Perfect dies. Rarity 4.

1798. B-9a

From same dies as B-9, but letters of LIBERTY are bifurcated, and there are die cracks as follows: A crack on obverse from border up through 17 to bust. Another crack from border through two lower points of second star. Other cracks from third to sixth stars. Reverse shows light break through STATES OF AM. Another break from border down through M to ribbon. Rarity 4.

1798. B-10 (H-10)

OBVERSE Spur on 9. Medium wide date, 10½ mm. across at bottom widest place. Die break upward from right portion of L in LIBERTY. Die flaw between point of last star and bust. Light die crack from border under 7 of date to left through several stars. Same obverse die used for B-13.

REVERSE 5 small berries, the two uppermost being closest together. Leaf points under left side of upright of I in AMERICA. Star [slightly] distant from eagle's beak. 13 perfect arrows. A die flaw under end of stem. All specimens examined show wear in die on eagle. Rarity 4.

1798. B-11

OBVERSE No spur on 9. Medium wide date, 10 mm. across at bottom widest place. First star about as far from curl as upper right star is from Y. The upper left star is closer to L in LIBERTY and about the same distance as last star is from bust. "Hill-shaped" die cutting shows just beneath ribbon bow along two highest curls at back of head.

REVERSE 5 small berries, the two upper ones closest together. The third berry from top is attached to a leaf point. A leaf points to space between R and I in AMERICA. Star is distant from eagle's beak. 13 perfect arrows. Same reverse die used for B-15, B-16, B-27.

Perfect dies. Unknown to Haseltine. The dies broke early. Rarity 6.

1798. B-11a (H-11)

From same dies as B-11, but with die break under chin across three points of last star to border. Another die break across hair above ear. This is the variety known to Haseltine. Rarity 3.

1798. B-11b

From same dies as last, but the die break across hair continues across cheek, mouth, and upper point of last star to border. Very rare. Rarity 5.

1798. B-12 (H-12)

OBVERSE 17 of date close together, other figures wider apart. A trifle more than 10 mm. across date at bottom widest part. First star distant 3½ mm. from curl. 1 near curl, 8 far from bust. Lips of Liberty open. Last star points to center of a denticle.

REVERSE Star touches lower part of eagle's beak. 5 small berries, 2 above closest together. Leaf points slightly right of center of I in AMERICA. 13 arrows. Die crack through UNITED ST and above AT. Same reverse die used for B-29. Rarity 4.

1798. B-13 (H-13)

OBVERSE From same die as B-10.

REVERSE *Only 10 arrows.* 5 small berries, 2 top ones closest together. Point of leaf under left lower tip of I in AMERICA. Star distant from eagle's beak. Die crack along right wing tip, top of AM to border above E. Same reverse die as B-21. A very common variety. Rarity 1.

1798. B-14 (H-14)

OBVERSE Medium wide date, 10¼ mm. across at bottom widest part. Spur on 9. The 1 in date close to hair, 8 close to bust. *Stars about equi-distant* from curl, L, Y, and bust, except that upper left star is a little closer to L. The first star points slightly left of center of a denticle. The highest curl on head s o l i d, and c e n t e r e d u n d e r upright of E. Some lines (suction marks) show in field between curl and first two stars. NOTE. This obverse die closely resembles B-24, which see.

REVERSE 5 small berries, two top ones closest together. Point of leaf un- der left lower point of I in AMERICA. Star just misses touching point of upper part of eagle's beak, and in worn speci- mens appears to touch. 13 perfect arrows. Rarity 3.

1798. B-14a

From same dies as B-14, but the die appears rough and raised inside of 6 stars on left, and a "tail" between 4th and 5th stars. Leaf under C is defective. Die flakes in E of UNITED. Rarity 6.

1798. B-14b

From same dies as B-14a, and with same die cracks, but the die break on obverse is now heavier, nearly obliterating the 7th star and part of L. A crack on reverse through right part of O. Rarity 5.

1798. B-15 (H-15)

OBVERSE Spur on 9. Wide date, 11 mm. across at bottom widest part. 7th star very close to L, slightly closer than figure 1 of date from curl. Last star slightly nearer bust than figure 8 is from bust. Lowest right star points to a space between two denticles.

REVERSE From same die as B-11. Rarity 2.

1798. B-15a

From same dies as B-15, but the stars appear smaller. Struck before the die was finished. Ex. rare. Rarity 5.

1798. B-16 (H-16)

OBVERSE Wide date, the most space between 98. The 8th star slightly closer to Y than 13th is to bust. The 7th star distant from L, and the first star a trifle farther from curl. The die broke early and so badly that very few pieces were struck, possibly not over two, as no others are known to the author. A number of pieces formerly attributed as H.16 in various catalogues and examined by the author, turned out to be incorrectly attributed. The die break is heavy and extends from border on left near first star to right through base of lowest curl and top of 179 of date. There is a spur downward from a denticle above right part of E in LIBERTY.

REVERSE From same die as B-11. Excessively rare. Rarity 8.

1798. B-17 (H-17)

OBVERSE   Very wide date, the 8 just touching bust.   Date is over 11½ mm. across at bottom widest part.   Upper star on left very close to L, and upper star on right is near Y.   Second star points slightly right of denticle.   The denticles to left of date are irregular.

REVERSE   From same die as B-6, but earlier impressions, when the berries were delicate and very small (smallest on any variety), having been later worked over in the die work for B-6.   On this variety some berries appear without stems.   Only 10 arrows, the two sticks having now been removed.

Excessively rare.   Haseltine's was only good, the only one he ever found.   The author's is fine, and the only one he has seen. Rarity 7.

1798. B-18 (H-18)

OBVERSE   Very wide date, 11 mm. across at widest part.   1 close to curl, 8 near bust but does not touch.   Two upper stars near L and Y. First star nearly 4 mm. from hair.   Last star points to left edge of a denticle. Die lump midway between center of date and bust.   Same obverse die used for B-20 and B-21.

REVERSE   *Die break* from milling down through right part of E to clouds. This break has been seen on all specimens examined.   Die breaks through last S in STATES and top of OF.   Light die crack from top of N to base of D in UNITED.   5 medium sized berries, the two top ones closest together.   Leaf point below lower left corner of I in AMERICA.   Star distant from eagle's beak. 13 arrows.   Same reverse die as B-22.

Excessively rare.   Rarity 8.

1798. B-19 (H-19)

OBVERSE   Very wide date, *distant from bust*.   Upper left star near L. Upper and lower right stars equi-distant from Y and bust.   First star points to lower edge of a denticle.   Vertical die break down through stand of E in LIBERTY, across bust through 1 of date to border.

REVERSE   Several die flaws, one between ST, another between TE, another at right of E in STATES.   Curved die flaw above third upper right star on reverse. 5 small berries, the two above closest together. Leaf point is under left point of I in AMERICA. Star distant from eagle's beak. 13 arrows. Same reverse die used for B-23. Very rare. Rarity 5.

1798. B-20 (H-20)

OBVERSE   From same die as B-18, and B-21.

REVERSE   From same die as B-3 and B-7. The die crack that developed on B-7 from right wing down through I in AMERICA to border has now become heavier. Another crack below ER in AMER-ICA. Rarity 4.

1798. B-21 (H-21)

OBVERSE   From same die as B-18 and B-20.

REVERSE   From same die as B-13. An extra "stick" is made to show with the 10 arrows. Rare variety. Rarity 4.

1798. B-22 (H-22)

OBVERSE   Very wide date, the 8 firmly united with bust. Spur on 9. This die is similar to B-17, but the upper stars, while near L and Y, are not as close to them as in B-17. Second star points to a space between two denticles, third to left part of a denticle. Slight die crack under Y and 8th and 9th stars, shows on some specimens. Same obverse die as B-23.

REVERSE   From same die as B-18. Rarity 2.

1798. B-23 (H-23)

OBVERSE   From same die as B-22.

REVERSE   From same die as B-19. Rarity 3.

1798. B-23a

From same dies as B-23, but rare variety with second curl from bottom defective, and letters in LIBERTY bifurcated. Rarity 4.

1798.   B-24 (H-24)

OBVERSE   This is an entirely new obverse die.   Capt. Haseltine in his list made in 1881, described this obverse as being from the same die as H-14.   However, this is one of the few errors he made in his work.   This die does *resemble* the obverse of B-14 more than any other.   In B-14 the 8 in date is about twice as close to bust as in B-24.   In B-24 the 11th and 12th stars are much farther apart than in B-14.   In B-24 the first two stars at lower left, point to the center of denticles.   In B-14 the second star points to left edge of a denticle.   Also in B-14 the highest curl on head is solid and under upright of E, while in B-24 this curl is sketchy and defective and a little more centered under E.

REVERSE   Also closely resembles that of B-14 as both have 5 small berries with two top ones closest together; both have 13 arrows.   However, in this number, the leaf points under left side of *upright* of I in AMERICA.   The star *touches* point of upper part of eagle's beak.   *Die break from stem* down to milling.   Two uppermost stars in center partly in clouds.   *Small die flaws* in E of STATES, between E and S, and under S.   Die crack from cloud under last S of STATES through top of O and down to base of F.   [Same reverse die used for B-25.]   A very common variety.   Rarity 1.

1798.   B-24a

From same dies as B-24, but die crack from neck through right field, 12th star, to border.   Another crack through lower 4 stars on right to bust.   Another crack from lowest curl through top of 798 to border under point of bust.   Small crack from border down to B.   Rarity 2.

1798.   B-25 (H-25)

OBVERSE   Close date, only 9½ mm. across at widest part.   "Whisker" on chin.   *Die dot* in field under chin, about one-third of the distance between neck and 12th star.   1 very close to curl.   Last star near bust, upper right star distant from Y, upper left star still farther from L, and first star farthest from curl.

REVERSE   From same die as B-24.   The die break from stem is lighter.

A rare variety.   Rarity 4.

1798.   B-25a

From same dies as B-25, but letters on reverse are bifurcated. The break from stem end has not yet developed. Die flaws in field between two upper stars on right on reverse show, as they do on all varieties from this die examined by me. Very rare. Rarity 5.

1798.   B-25b

From same dies as B-25, but with extensive die breaks all around obverse. (See plate) The break on reverse at stem is heavy like on B-24. Rarity 4.

1798.   B-26 (H-26)

OBVERSE — Close date, about 9½ mm. at widest part. *The 8 much too high,* and out of position, top leaning to right. Die flaw like a horizontal line close to inner point of 12th star.

This same obverse die with the above distinguishing features was used for B-27, B-28, B-29, B-30, and B-31, and all sub-varieties. On this particular variety, a light die break starts at border under 9 through two inner points of first star ending in field.

REVERSE — *Point of star touches point of upper part of eagle's beak.* 12 arrows and a stick. One of these arrows, the nearest one to N has a very small head. (Haseltine called this the 11-arrow variety.) There are 5 small berries, the two at top closest together. Point of leaf under center of I in AMERICA. *Die break* from shield to border below, passes through end of stem. Light die crack through top of ES, base of O, right cloud, right wing and ribbon, outer leaves of branch, lower part of A and stem end, thence through eagle's tail. The two upper center stars touch clouds. Rarity 2.

1798.   B-27 (H-27)

OBVERSE — From same die as B-26, but without the die break under 9 and left.

REVERSE — From same die as B-11, B-15, and B-16. In this combination, a light die break appears through top of S OF and right wing tip. Rarity 2.

1798.   B-28 (H-28)

OBVERSE   From same die as B-26, but the die break is more pronounced; it continues from first star to hair ribbon.   Additional break up through 9 to bust, and one along border to right base of bust. From same die as used for B-26, B-28, B-29, B-30, B-31, the die cracks similar to B-30 and B-31.

REVERSE   Leaf point is slightly right of center of I in AMERICA.   Star distant from eagle's beak.   13 perfect arrows.   5 medium-sized berries, the two at top closest together.

A die crack begins at border above last S in STATES, and passes through center of OF, right wing, bottom of AME, up through RIC.   Short crack from last A to border, another from lower outside leaf of branch past claw to stem end.   Heavy break from lower left part of shield down through claw and arrow butts. Another die break through U and left wing.   Another crack through NITE up through TA.   (See plate.)   Rarity 3.

1798.   B-29 (H-29)

OBVERSE   From same die as B-26, B-27, B-28, B-30, and B-31.   In this variety the die break is similar to those on B-28 but more advanced, now extending across bust into right field.   Two short cracks from bust to last star.   Additional crack from outside first star through next 3 stars and passing under the 5th, 6th, and 7th stars.

REVERSE   From same die as B-12.   (See plate.)   Rarity 3.

1798.   B-30 (H-30)

OBVERSE   From same die as B-26, B-27, B-28, B-29, B-31.   The die cracks on this variety are the same as on B-28.

REVERSE   The upper stars on reverse are all very *distant from clouds.* Leaf points to space between R and I in AMERICA.   Point of star barely touches upper part of eagle's beak.   13 perfect arrows.   5 small berries, 2 at top nearest together.   See plate. Rarity 5.

1798. B-30a

From same dies as B-30, but with numerous die breaks on reverse, and heavy break through upper left part of first A in AMERICA to border. Die cracks through AM down to wing, base of R through branch and shield, top of R through ICA, lower part of UNITE, and another through TED to wing, top of D STA. Extremely rare. Rarity 6.

1798. B-31 (New)

OBVERSE — From same die as B-26, B-27, B-28, B-29, and B-30. The die cracks on this variety are similar to those on B-28 and B-30.

REVERSE — A new reverse die, unknown to Haseltine. *Star close to both* upper and lower points of eagle's beak but does not touch. Leaf points near center of upright of I in AMERICA. 5 small berries, the two upper ones closest together. 13 perfect arrows. Slight die break along upper side of right wing tip. Excessively rare. Rarity 7.

1798. B-31a

Same as B-31, but variety with extensive die breaks on reverse. (See plate.) Heavy break from border down through right side of O, top of F to wing, down to cloud below, from border at right wing tip through A under MERICA across claw, stem, & tail; continuing under UNI, across bottom of TED, left wing tip, center of STA. Also four curved die breaks down from TES through stars. Excessively rare. Rarity 7.

1798. B-32 (New)

OBVERSE — From same die as B-1.

REVERSE — From same die as B-4.

1798. B-33 (New)

OBVERSE — From the same die as B-26 through B-31, with the die in the same condition as B-28 as to the die cracks, one of which is quite obvious, under the date to the first star.

REVERSE — A new reverse die, unknown to Haseltine or Bolender. Point of star almost touches upper beak. No stars touch clouds, although the last is very close. 13 perfect arrows. 4 small berries, 1 large berry, upper two closest together. Point of leaf left of center of I in AMERICA.

Heavy die break bisects the die from 8 o'clock to 3 o'clock Weakly struck on lower obverse. Rust pits in shield.

[41]

THE SILVER DOLLARS OF 1799

IN the year 1799 a total of 423,515 silver dollars were struck from 12 different obverse dies, and 17 reverse dies combined so as to make no less than twenty-two distinct varieties. Besides, there are many die cracks and other peculiarities, some of which also have been listed as sub-varieties to aid in the classification as well as to add pleasure to this fascinating collecting. The issue was the largest of any year from 1794 to 1803, the period of the "lettered edge" dollars. However, this issue was a small one, when you consider that in only one year since, over fifty million were coined.[1]

It is interesting to note that my numbers 5, 6, 7, 10, 11, and 17 are all from the same obverse die, but vary in the refinishing work of the engraver, and show various stages of die cracks. Nos. 5, 7, 10, and 17 usually show suction marks that appear as "waves" above the date.

The 1799 reverses can better be classified with the following helps.

THE BERRIES —

Numbers 11 and 12 have *no berries* in branch.
No. 15 has 5 *small* berries, the only small berry variety.
No. 17 has 5 *extra large* berries, the two upper ones *joined* to leaves.
All other numbers have 5 large berries, with the two top berries closest together.

THE POINT OF LEAF UNDER I IN AMERICA —

Between left corner and left side of upright — 10, 17
Left side of upright — 2, 3, 4, 11, 12, 15, 16, 18, 19, 23
Slightly right of left upright — 5
Center of upright — 1, 6, 7, 13, 14, 21
Slightly right of center — 8, 22
Right side of upright — 9

POSITION OF STAR AND EAGLE'S BEAK

Star touches lower part of beak — 1, 2, 5, 6, 8, 9, 10, 11, 12, 14, 16, 18, 19, 21, 22, 23
Star touches upper part of beak — 7, 15, 17
Star very close to beak, barely escaping touching upper part — 3, 4, 13

[1] At the Philadelphia mint in 1922.

POSITION OF SAME STAR (Lowest left on reverse) DOWNWARD POINT TOWARD B & U IN PLURIBUS

Star points to space between B and U — 7, 8, 14, 17, 21
Star points to left upright of U — 3, 4, 5, 6, 9, 10, 22
Star points to right side of left upright of U — 2, 19
Star points slightly left of left upright of U — 1, 11, 12, 16, 23
Star points to right side of B — 13, 15

POSITION OF FIRST A IN AMERICA

Touches 4th feather — 2, 13, 16, 19, 23
Touches 3rd feather — 5, 7, 9, 22
Touches both 3rd and 4th feathers — 1, 6
Touches no feathers — 3, 4, 8, 10, 11, 12, 14, 15, 17, 18, 20, 21

1799 OBVERSES

Numbers	First Star	7th Star	8th Star	13th Star
1, 2, 3	Farthest	About equal to 13th	Distant	About equal to 7th
4, 13, 15	Farthest		Near	One point just touches bust
5, 6, 7, 10, 11, 17	Farthest	Almost as near as 8th	Slightly closest	Not as near bust as upper left is to L
8, 12	Farthest	Slightly closer to L than 8th is to Y		Distant from bust
9	About 2 mm.	7th & 8th closest and about equal		About 1½ mm. from bust
14, 22	Farthest	Farther from L than 8th from Y		Slightly closer to bust than 8th to Y
16	About same distance from curl as 7th is from L		Slightly closer Y than 13th from bust	
18, 19	About same as 7th & 13th	About same as 1st & 13th	Farthest	About same as 1st & 7th
21	Farthest	Second nearest	Much the closest	almost 2 mm.
23	Only 5 stars to right of bust			

THIS TABLE will help to more quickly identify varieties of 1799 obverses. With it study the comparative distances of lower left (first) star from curl, upper left (7th) star from L in LIBERTY, upper right (8th) star from Y, and lower right (13th) star from bust.

1799 SILVER DOLLARS (Quick Finding List)

Number

1   Over '98. Reverse die breaks above and to left of I in AMERICA.

2   Over '98. Reverse die break through curved part of D in UNITED.

3   Over '98. Reverse 15 stars, the two extra ones almost buried in clouds, just the points showing. The one at extreme left is easiest seen.

4   Irregular date, last star touches bust. 15-star reverse.

5   "Waves" at top of date, "pocket" under throat of Liberty. Rx. U in UNITED cut off at upper left corner.

6   First star smaller than others. A in STATES touches clouds.

7   "Waves" above date, "pocket" at throat. Rx. first A in AMERICA touches 3rd feather, only. Star touches upper part of eagle's beak.

8   Open mouth Liberty. Die flaws inside and to right of top of final S in STATES. A line between N and I in UNITED at base.

9   Obv. die flaws in field under I extending downward toward ribbon. Rx. "apostrophe" after final S in STATES. Leaf point under right side of upright of I in AMERICA.

10   Leaf point between left corner and left side of upright of I in AMERICA. 5 large berries, 2 upper ones closest together.

11   8th star closer to Y than 7th is to L. No berries.

12   7th star closer to L than 8th is to Y. No berries.

13   Irregular date, last star touches bust. Rx. die dot above E in STATES.

14   Two die flaws in field before eye. Rx. die flaws under AM, and between two lower stars just back of eagle's head.

15   Irregular date, last star touches bust. Rx. 5 small berries.

16   Left stars distant from curl and L. Right stars close to Y and bust. Rx. upper left corner off U in UNITED.

17   5 very large berries, the two upper ones partly buried in leaves.

18   8th star farther from Y than 1st from curl or 7th from L or 13th from bust. Rx. heavy die break between ED and through left wing.

19   Same obverse as last, but broken die. Rx. die break through curved part of D in UNITED.

21   8th star much closer to Y than 1st star to curl, or 7th star to L, or 13th star to bust. Rx. die flaws under AM.

22   Die flaw in field before eye. Horizontal die crack entirely across reverse.

23   Only 5 stars to right of bust, facing.

[45]

1799. B-1 (H-1)

OBVERSE 1799 over '98. Last 9 of date very close to bust. Stars very close together. Letters of LIBERTY are widely spaced. Die flaw at left base of E, [under RT, and above R.] Same die used for B-2 and B-3.

REVERSE Leaf points to center of I in AMERICA. Star touches point of *lower part of eagle's beak*. First A in AMERICA touches 3rd feather, and rests on fourth. Die cracked and scaled between R and I in AMERICA, above same I, and above right part of first T in STATES. Slight die crack sometimes shows through bottom of ES up to top of O, another through lower part of OF. Very rare. Rarity 5.

1799. B-2 (H-2)

OBVERSE 1799 over '98. From same die as B-1 and B-3. Die flaws as on B-1.

REVERSE Die break from border down through *curved part of D* and showing at base. Leaf point is below left side of upright of I in AMERICA. The E in AMERICA is defective at top. Star touches lower part of eagle's beak and *just enters the mouth*. A touches 4th feather, but not the third. Same reverse die used for B-19. Rarity 4.

1799. B-3 (H-3)

OBVERSE 1799 over '98. From same die as B-1 and B-2.

REVERSE *The "15-star reverse"*. There are two extra stars almost buried in the clouds, with just the points showing. The one at extreme left is the most easily seen. Leaf point under left upright of I in America. Die crack near border above ATES. Another crack above OF AM, another from right ribbon up through E and top of RIC. Same reverse die used for B-4. Rarity 5.

1799. B-4 (H-4)

OBVERSE *Irregular date*. Both 9's are improperly placed, the first 9 is tipped too far to left at top, the last 9 too far to right at top. *A point of last star touches bust*. Same obverse die used for B-13 and B-15, and comes with and without various stages of die breaks. This specimen has numerous die cracks all around obverse. See plate.

REVERSE   From same die as B-3.   Rarity 4.

1799.   B-5 (H-5)

OBVERSE   *Light waves* (suction marks) appear at top of date between two 9's and to right.   Letters in LIBERTY close, and slightly bifurcated.   First star appears small and thin.   *"Pocket" under throat* of Liberty shows on B-5, B-6, and B-7.   The *closest star* is the 8th star which is slightly closer to Y, than 7th star is to L. First star slightly farther from curl than last star is from bust. In B-5 and B-6 the upper right corner is slightly off 1 in date. Same obverse die with slight corrections used for B-6, B-7, B-10, B-11, & B-17.

REVERSE   U in UNITED *imperfect at upper left,* the thick part being cut off at upper left corner.   This also happened on B-16, although it is a different die.   Leaf points almost under left side of upright of I in AMERICA.   All six upper stars touch clouds, the two on right each having two points touching, and other four have one point touching.   Point of star touches point of lower part of eagle's beak.   Another point of same star points to left park of U in PLURIBUS.   A touches third feather.   Common variety. Rarity 2.

1799.   B-5a

From same dies as B-5.   Obverse short die cracks from lower left corner of E down to hair, and below first star.   Reverse die crack through UNITED STATES.   Rarity 3.

1799.   B-6 (H-6)

OBVERSE   From same die as B-5, B-7, B-10, B-11, and B-17.   This specimen shows a slight crack along border opposite point of bust.

REVERSE   A in STATES touches clouds.   Leaf points to center of upright of I in AMERICA.   Letter A touches both 3rd and 4th feathers. Point of star touches lower part of eagle's beak.   Upper stars about same as B-5, except that the second star from the left has two points touching clouds. AME joined at lower part. Very rare. Rarity 5.

1799. B-7 (H-7)

OBVERSE From same die is B-5, B-6, B-10, B-11, and B-17. In this combination or "marriage" to this reverse die, the top of 1 in date is refinished and straight cut. The "throat pocket" still shows, as do the "waves" at top of date.

REVERSE Point of star touches point of upper part of eagle's beak. First A in AMERICA touches third feather only. Leaf points near center of upright of I in AMERICA. Upper star at extreme left has two points touching clouds. Rarity 4.

1799. B-7a

From same dies as B-7, but variety with die breaks through lower part of UNITED, center of STA, bottom of TES, lower part of AMERICA. Rarity 5.

1799. B-8 (H-8)

OBVERSE Liberty with open mouth. First star is slightly farther from curl than last star is from bust, or about 2 mm. from curl. The 7th star is slightly closer to L than 8th star is to Y. Letters in LIBERTY are much bifurcated. Highest curl on top of head is centered more under *right half* of E in LIBERTY, while on Nos. 5, 6, & 7 the curl is centered more *under left half* of E. The 1 in date is much farther from the curl, slightly over 1 mm. This obverse closely resembles B-12, which see.

REVERSE *Die flaws* inside and to right top of final S in STATES. Point of star touches point of lower part of eagle's beak. Leaf points slightly right of center of I in AMERICA. A line between N and I in UNITED at base. AME join at lowest part. Rarity 3.

1799. B-8a

From same dies as B-8, but with die break from border through two points of seventh star and LIB. Rarity 3.

1799. B-8b

From same dies as B-8, with die breaks as in B-8a, but crack is heavier through LIBE and extends farther. Additional break from border above T down through TY. Top of E and R defective. The reverse die is now badly shattered with numerous breaks. The die breaks *cross* in top of final S of STATES. Rare. Rarity 5.

1799. B-9 (H-9)

OBVERSE Similar to B-5, but from a different die. The stars are larger, making them closer together. The upper left and right stars are about equi-distant from L and Y. 13th star about 1½ mm. from bust. First star about 2 mm. from curl. Letters in LIBERTY are slightly bifurcated. *Die flaws* in field under I extending downward toward ribbon. This specimen shows a very faint die crack from top of first 9 in date across bust, touching chin, to point of 10th star.

REVERSE "Apostrophe" after final S in STATES. Star touches point of lower part of eagle's beak. Leaf points under right side of upright of I in AMERICA. A touches 3rd feather only. Die break through MERIC.

This is by far the most common variety of the year. Rarity 1.

1799. B-9a

From same dies as B-9, but variety with more fine cracks on obverse. A crack joins 9th & 10th stars. Crack from under T joins other break in field before nose. "Waves" appear above date. Rarity 2.

1799. B-10 (H-10)

OBVERSE From same die as B-5, B-6, B-7, B-11, and B-17. In this combination the "pocket" under throat has been removed, corrected in the die. Upper side of 1 in date is a straight line. This specimen shows a light die crack through last three stars.

REVERSE Leaf point between left corner and left side of upright of I in AMERICA. Farthest arrow point is under right upright of N. Point of star enters eagle's mouth, and touches lower part of eagle's beak. Another point of same star points to left upright of

U in PLURIBUS. Die break from border through OF, bottom of AMERICA, eagle's tail, arrows, left wing, up through ST, top of AT. Rarity 2.

1799. B-10a

From same dies as B-10, but a die crack appears on obverse through last four stars. Reverse has additional die cracks through ATES, three cracks from clouds down among stars, and two cracks form a cross in O. Another crack through right ribbon, branch, and eagle's tail. Rarity 3.

1799. B-10b

From same dies as B-10, without obverse crack of B-10a, but with reverse cracks as in 10a, and with letters much bifurcated. Rarity 3.

1799. B-11 (H-11)

OBVERSE   From same die as B-10, perfect die. This die also used for B-5, B-6, B-7, B-11, and B-17.

REVERSE   *One tiny berry* in olive branch. Upper star on far left on reverse much smaller than any of the other stars. Left top of U defective. Same reverse die as used for B-12. Rarity 4.

1799. B-11a

From same dies as B-11, but sub-variety with heavy die break from border just touching right side of D in UNITED to fourth feather of wing. Very rare. Rarity 5.

1799. B-12 (H-12)

OBVERSE   Described by Haseltine as from same die as H-9, but it is from a different die. (This one of Haseltine's few errors in his arduous work.) This new die closely resembles both B-8 and B-9, but the first star is much *farther from curl,* slightly over 2½ mm. (Only about 2 mm. in B-9) Letters in LIBERTY are only very slightly bifurcated.

REVERSE   *No berries.* From same die as B-11. Perfect dies. Rarity 3.

1799. B-12a

From same dies as B-12, but obverse shows *light die breaks* from border below 7, through bottom of figure 1, ending in left field. A crack from bottom of first 9 to border below. Fine crack from center of 7 through base of both 9's. Fine crack at right of date, border to bust. Rarity 4.

1799. B-12b

Same as B-12a, but the die breaks there described are now more pronounced, and several other breaks show up thus shattering the die and terminating its use. Two breaks across hair and bust. A break from 9th star curves through field to border near point of bust. Die break from neck joins this crack. Reverse perfect die. See plate. Rarity 4.

1799. B-13 (H-13)

OBVERSE   From same die as B-4 and B-15.   Perfect die without die breaks.

REVERSE   *Die "dot"* above E in STATES, and *die flaws* inside upper part of same letter. Die flaws also appear between and under two lower stars farthest to right. Star is close to eagle's beak, and barely escapes touching its upper part. Another point of same star points down to right side of B in PLURIBUS. Leaf points to center of I in AMERICA. A touches fourth feather of right wing. Extremely rare. Rarity 6.

1799. B-14 (H-14)

OBVERSE   *Two die flaws* in field before eye, one very clear. Last star near bust (about ½ mm.) and a little closer than 8th star is to Y. 7th star farther from L, and first star nearly 2 mm. from curl. Last three stars point to spaces between denticles. The last 9 is about as near bust as upper right star is to Y. *Die flaw* from outer point of 10th star. Same obverse die used for B-22.

REVERSE   *Die flaws* under AM and between two lower stars just back of eagle's head. Point of star touches point of lower part of eagle's beak. Another point of same star points to space between B and U of PLURIBUS. Leaf points to center of I in AMERICA. A does not touch feathers of right wing, but is near 3rd feather.

[51]

Die crack through upper part of AME. From same die as B-21. Rarity 4.

1799. B-15 (H-15)

OBVERSE
From same die as B-4 and B-13. Irregular date. This specimen shows a light die crack through first four stars and toward date.

REVERSE
Reverse of 1798. Struck from the same die as B-24 of the 1798 dollars! [The 5 berries are the smallest of any variety of this date.] A die break joins stem end to border below. Very rare variety. Rarity 5.

1799. B-15a

From same dies as B-15, but numerous additional die breaks. A break through lower part of date passes through all stars on left. Another crack from hair to first star. Another break from upper left star through LIBE. Break from border above R down through RT to nose. Break through top of Y and three upper stars on right. Rare. Rarity 4.

1799. B-16 (H-16)

OBVERSE
Left stars distant from curl and L. *Right stars close* to Y and bust. This die is quickly recognized by keeping the above in mind. The first star is about 2 mm. distant from curl, and the 7th star is just as far from the L. The 8th star is quite close to Y, and the last star almost as near to bust.

REVERSE
U in UNITED defective at upper left part, which is cut off. Point of star touches point of lower part of eagle's beak. A point of same star points down to left side of U in PLURIBUS. A in AMERICA rests on 4th feather. Leaf point is under left side of upright of I. Upper right star has *only one point* touching cloud. Die used for B-23. Rarity 2.

1799. B-16a

From same dies as B-16, but "waves" above date. Suction marks (outlines of clouds and eagle's wing of reverse) show between stars on left to stars on right of obverse. The reverse shows a die break from cloud up through OF to top of wing. Same as B-23 reverse.

1799. B-16b

From same dies as B-16, but with numerous die cracks shattering the dies. Crack from border to inner points of first star; from border through 2 upper points of first star through hair and bust down to milling after date. Crack from border through lowest curl and above date. Another crack joins this crack left of date passing up through curls and ribbon in two cracks to 5th and 6th stars. Cracks from nose through 9th star. Another crack through front of bust up into field. Crack through inner points of last star.

Reverse same as B-16a, but two cracks up through OF. I have seen only one. Extremely rare variety. Rarity 6.

1799. B-17 (M-17)

OBVERSE From same die as B-5, B-6, B-7, B-10, and B-11. Most similar to B-10 with the "throat pocket" at junction of chin and neck removed. The die crack shows through last 4 stars. A faint crack near border opposite point of bust.

REVERSE *5 extra large berries* in olive branch. The two upper berries are partly buried in the leaves. Point of star enters eagle's mouth, upper part of beak closing down on star. The point of the star almost touches lower part of beak. Another point of same star points down to space between B and U of PLURI-BUS. Leaf points near left corner of I in AMERICA. A does not touch feathers. Very short stem in claw. Peculiar *die flaws* under second upper star from left. Rarity 2.

1799. B-17a

From same dies as B-17, but reverse die crack from border through center of U, bottom of NITED, left wing, up through ST. Rare. Rarity 4.

1799. B-18 (H-18)

OBVERSE 8th star farther from Y than the first star from curl, or the 7th star from L, or the last star from bust. Highest curl on top of head is centered under right edge of E and space between E and R. Same die used for B-19.

REVERSE *Heavy die break* between E and D through left wing, to top of shield. Lighter breaks usually through TATES O, from lower part of F to top of A, from border above R, top of I, through CA, stem end, tail, up through NIT. Small point at stem end. A does not touch feathers. Leaf points below left side of upright of I in AMERICA. Point of star touches lower point of eagle's beak. Extremely rare. Rarity 6.

1799. B-19 (H-19)

OBVERSE From same die as B-18, but with die break from border under bust, through bottom of last 9, center of 179, and first three stars on left to border. Another crack from second star to hair.

REVERSE From same die as B-2. Very rare. Rarity 5.

NOTE. Haseltine's No. 20 was only a perfect die impression of No. 18, and is not a distinct die variety. Thus, No. 20 does not exist, and is now omitted to make my numbers coincide with Haseltine's.

1799. B-21 (H-21)

OBVERSE 8th star much closer to Y than first star to curl, or 7th star to L, or last star to bust. First star is farthest from hair. 1 close to curl. Slight die roughness below first star, between milling and curl. This specimen shows die cracks down through 7 to milling, up through both 9's, bust, all stars on right, RTY. Another crack up through bust into field.

REVERSE From same die as B-14. Rare variety. Rarity 4.

1799. B-22 (H-22)

OBVERSE From same obverse die as B-14. Die flaw in field before eye.

REVERSE *Horizontal die break* entirely across center of reverse, from right side of E to left side of M. One arrow extends slightly past right side of upright of N. Star touches lower point of eagle's beak, and another point of same star points to left stand of U in PLURIBUS. Leaf point is slightly right of being under center of I in AMERICA.   Letter A touches only 3rd feather.   Extremely rare variety.   Rarity 6.

1799.   B-23   (H-23)

OBVERSE   *Only 5 stars* to right of bust, facing.   There are 8 stars on left side back of bust.

REVERSE   From same die as B-16.   The three upper berries are very small, and appear larger on B-16, refinishing work of the engraver. Rarity 5.

THE BRASHER COUNTERSTAMPED DOLLAR
OF 1799

1799 U.S. Silver Dollar (B-8a) *counterstamped* by Ephraim Brasher, New York City merchant, famous for his Brasher gold doubloons. With counterstamp EB in depressed rectangle, on top part of head. Excessively rare. From the celebrated Dunham collection.

THE SILVER DOLLARS OF 1800

IN the year 1800 a total of 220,920 silver dollars were coined, using no less than 12 different obverse dies and 11 different reverse dies in various combinations to produce at least seventeen distinct varieties. Besides, a study of the various stages of die breaks proves to be fascinating, offering more interest in the series before it can be completed.

The quick-finding list that follows is intended to help the collector and busy dealer to more quickly attribute any coin. The distinguishing features are given in this list briefly. In a moment you will have a clue. Then turn to the detailed description under that number and check the description, as well as the plates, being careful to consider both obverse and reverse.

1800 SILVER DOLLARS (Quick-finding List)

Number

1   In date 180 close. Die flaws near inside point 11th star. First T in STATES is double-cut.

2   R IN LIBERTY *and* first T in STATES double-cut.

3   R in LIBERTY double-cut. Leaf about touches center of lower stand of I in AMER-ICA. Letters AME do not join, but are close.

4   In date, 1 close to curl, 8 tipped to right. T in UNITED double-cut. AME join.

5   Die dot inside *lower* part of R in LIBERTY. Upper left star closest. AM join. Leaf under left side of upright of I in AMERICA.

8   Die dot inside lower part of R in LIBERTY. Upper left star closest. AM do not join. Leaf slightly left of center of I.

10   Very wide date, 8 low. AM join.

11   Very wide date, 8 low. AM do not join, but ME almost join. AMERICAI.

12   R in LIBERTY double-cut *and* a dot inside lower part of E in UNITED. 5 *small* berries. AME do not join.

13   Wide even date. 13th star closest, then the 8th almost as near Y. 7th star much farther from L, and first star farthest from hair. AM touch.

14   So-called "dotted date", flaws inside and above first O. ME join. Only 12 arrows show plainly, 13th nearly hidden.

15   Last star very close to bust. Dot between RT. Only 10 arrows.

16   Close date, 1 almost touches curl. Die dot to left of top curl on head.

17   "Collar" along neck in front. A line to left from foot of 1 in date. 12 arrows.

18   Last star closest, and nearer bust than 8th star is to Y. Die break like a spray from right wing through F, clouds, stars.

19   Stars close to Y and bust. Vertical die flaw below right side of first star near border. AMERICAI.

20   Upper right star has two points close to Y, the upper point nearly touching. T in UNITED double-cut.

1800. B-1 (H-1)

OBVERSE   180 close in date. TY too far apart. The 1 in date *barely misses* touching the hair. Slight *elevation* in field between lowest left star and hair. *Die flaws* near inside point of 11th star and also at lower outside of same star. 8th star near Y, and last star near bust, the two about equi-distant.

REVERSE   *Leaf touches* lowest right corner of I in AMERICA Point of star touches point of lower part of eagle's beak. A in AMERICA touches only 3rd feather. First T in STATES is *double-cut*. AME joined at lower part. Same die as B-2. Haseltine listed it as just "scarce" but my records over a period of forty years show it to be extremely rare. Rarity 5.

1800. B-2 (H-2)

OBVERSE   Medium wide date, figures evenly spaced. Upper point of 8th star is very close to top right tip of Y. The R in LIBERTY is *double-cut*. Same obverse die used for B-3 and B-12.

REVERSE   From same die as B-1. Haseltine was in error in describing this reverse as differing from No. 1. It is a break in the die that "joins the A" to the fourth feather, and this break continues to border. There is also a slight crack through OF to wing. Haseltine had seen but a single specimen (this is probably the one), and I have seen but this one specimen. Rarity 7.

1800. B-3 (H-3)

OBVERSE   From same die as B-2 and B-12.

REVERSE   *Leaf touches center* of lower stand of I in AMERICA. The two upper stars on the right do not touch the clouds; the other stars each have one point touching. Point of star enters eagle's mouth, *not touching* lower part of beak. End of branch curves toward eagle's tail. AME close but do not join. A touches both 3rd and 4th feathers. Haseltine found but one (very fair) and it was 1949 before I found my only specimen. Rarity 8.

1800. B-4 (H-4)

OBVERSE   1 in date close to curl, and 8 tipped too much to right at top. Liberty's mouth open. 7th, 8th, and 13th stars are all equi-distant from L, Y and bust, and are near. First star about 2½ mm. distant from hair. This specimen shows slight die crack from border below 1 of date, through base of 1, upward through 8 to first 0. Another fine crack from border under first 0 through base of second 0 to bust.

REVERSE

Die flaws show at top and to right of ES, easily identifying this die which was also used for B-16 and B-20. The eagle's beak closes down on extreme point of a star. Leaf points slightly right of center of I in AMERICA. Letter T in UNITED is *double-cut*. From same reverse die as B-16 and B-20. Rare variety. Rarity 4.

1800. B-4a

From same dies as B-4, but with extensive die breaks on obverse. Die crack from border up through entire 1 of date and bust to 12th star. Another break through first star to curl under ribbon. Another break between IB touching left lower part of B down through hair. Crack along inner points of 10th to 12th stars. Very rare. Rarity 5.

1800. B-5 (H-5)

OBVERSE

Look for the die "dot" inside lower part of R in LIBERTY. This easily distinguishes this die, which was also used for B-8. Mouth of Liberty closed. Upper left star is closer to L than any of the other "key stars", the 8th star being a little more distant from Y, the 13th star still farther from bust, and the first star much farther from hair. The 1 is not very close to curl. The letters in LIBERTY are not bifurcated. Same die used for B-8.

REVERSE

A die flaw just to left of lower part of second T in STATES quickly identifies this reverse, the die also used for B-10. Star enters eagle's mouth, the upper part of beak touching star. All the stars above firmly touch clouds, except the second upper one from right which is very close. Leaf points under left side of upright of I. The A touches both 3rd and 4th feathers, AM joined at lower part. Some letters just slightly bifurcated. Same reverse die used for B-10. Rarity 4.

1800. B-5a

From same dies as B-5, but letters are much bifurcated, and all the figures of date also show the unfinished die work, all the figures being defective. Very rare. Rarity 5.

1800. B-5b

From same dies as B-5, with a die crack connecting upper three stars on left and top of LIB. Rarity 6.

NOTE. It is my opinion that Haseltine's No. 6 was only a worn specimen of his No. 5, and that No. 6 does not exist as a distinct die variety. Neither does No. 7 exist as a distinct die variety, but the variety mentioned by Capt. Haseltine under this number is my B-5a which was from the same die as H-5. The specimen listed in the sale of the "World's Greatest Collection" as "H-7" in Jan. 1945 was purchased by me, and upon close examination proved to be number 5a, and not a new die. Several others listed a H-6 and H-7 turned out to be wrongly attributed.

1800. B-8 (H-8)

OBVERSE From same die as B-5.

REVERSE Three upper stars on right on reverse *do not touch* clouds. Three upper stars on left on reverse each have *one point* touching clouds. Leaf points slightly left of center of I in AMERICA. Star enters eagle's mouth, upper part of beak closing down on side of star point. Letter A just touches 3rd and 4th feathers. AME do not join each other. Very large berries. Letters slightly bifurcated. Rarity 2.

NOTE. Haseltine's No. 9 was described by him as being struck from the dies used for No. 8, but with letters bifurcated. It therefore is *not a separate die variety,* but can be listed as a sub-variety as 8a.

1800. B-10 (H-10)

OBVERSE *Wide date, 00 very wide apart, and the 8 too low.* The 8th star is close to Y, last star not quite so near bust. The 7th star is distant from L, the first star still farther from hair. Highest curl on top of head defective. Same obverse die used for B-11.

REVERSE From same die as B-5, but with *light* die break from leaf through C to border. Rarity 2.

1800. B-10a

From same dies as B-10, but the die crack on reverse is more pronounced through C, and an additional crack extends from right ribbon end through ER. Rarity 3.

1800. B-11 (H-11)

OBVERSE From same die as B-10.

REVERSE AMERICAI variety. After the word AMERICA, an almost vertical line appears like an "I" added. Easy to distinguish this reverse, therefore, but remember that it was also used for B-19. Star enters eagle's mouth; point of lower part of beak touches star lightly below point. Upper part of beak does not quite touch. Point of leaf slightly right of being under left upright of I in AMERICA. Middle berry is small and joined to a leaf point. A touches 3rd feather only, and ME almost join at bottom. Excessively rare variety. It took me 35 years to find a specimen! Several times I found them listed as "H-11" but they always turned out to be H-19, which is struck from the same reverse die. Rarity 7.

1800. B-12 (H-12)

OBVERSE From same die as B-2 and B-3. The R in LIBERTY is double-cut. The stars are well-filled.

REVERSE A die dot inside lower part of E in UNITED, and a more prominent die flaw at lower left side of E in AMERICA. These things quickly distinguish this reverse from all others. The berries are small. Leaf point under left side of upright of I in AMERICA. Point of upper part of eagle's beak shuts down near point of star. A does not touch feathers, and AME do not join. Rarity 2.

1800. B-12a

From same dies as B-12, but reverse die shows die break across top of OF and right wing tip. Another crack from milling down through center of F. Rarity 3.

1800. B-13 (H-13)

OBVERSE   13th star slightly closer to bust than 8th star is from Y. The 7th star is much farther from L, and the first star is the farthest from hair, 2¾ mm. A wide evenly spaced date. From same obverse die as B-18.

REVERSE   Similar to B-8, but A and M touch. Two of the upper stars do not touch the clouds so decidedly. The branch is directed more towards the eagle's tail. Rarity 6.

1800. B-14 (H-14)

OBVERSE   *Dotted date,* that is, curious die flaws inside and above first 0 in date. Die flaws appear in many other places, particularly between L and I, under nose, before chin, below first star, and under the 6th and 7th stars. The 8th star closer to Y than last star from bust. The 7th star is a little farther from L, and the first star very distant from hair, over 3 mm.

REVERSE   *Only 12 arrows* show plainly, the 13th arrow much smaller and almost hidden. Leaf points to center of I in AMERICA. Point of star touches point of *lower part* of eagle's beak, and point of upper part of beak shuts down on top side of same star point. All upper stars touch clouds decidedly, except the second from right which barely misses. Die dot between second and third upper stars from right. ME join at base. Rarity 3.

1800. B-14a

From same dies as B-14, but with the following die breaks. Heavy die break under first 0 in date, up through left top of second 0 to bust. Break through right side of last 0 from milling to bust. Break from lower part of last 0, bust, and ending in right field. Light breaks in first 3 stars.

Reverse die breaks also appear from border, through right top of N into field. A break from milling to right top of E, base of D, left wing, lower part of clouds, continues in several cracks up through OF. Another break from top of D through left wing to S. Rarity 3.

1800. B-15 (H-15)

OBVERSE   *Last star very close to bust;* a point barely escapes touching the junction of drapery with bosom. The 1 in date is very close to curl, but does not touch. Figures 180 are close, and the last 0 more distant. Upper left star is near L. Die dot between R and T. The first star is very distant from hair, 4 mm.

REVERSE   *Only 10 perfect arrows* and 3 arrow heads *without sticks.* Numerous die flaws in TES and especially between last S of STATES and O. A does not touch feathers. AME join at base, the left base of M high and overlapping A. Star very close but does not quite touch eagle's beak. Rare variety. Rarity 4.

1800. B16 (H-16)

OBVERSE   Close date, 1 almost touches curl. The 8 is too low, and top tipped too much to right. Last 0 near bust. *Die dot just to left of highest curl* on top of head. Die flaws *between top* of R and T in LIBERTY. A fine curved die crack up through right side of final 0 in date, bust, point of chin, to 10th star.

REVERSE   From same die as B-4 and B-20. The T in UNITED is double-cut same as on B-4. Letters not bifurcated, on this specimen. Rarity 2.

1800. B-16a

From same dies as B-16, but with most letters bifurcated. Rarity 2.

1800. B-16b

From same dies as B-16, but variety showing suction marks as "waves" along top of date. Rarity 3.

1800. B-17 (H-17)

OBVERSE   *A "collar" shows along neck* (see plate) about half the length of bust. A *line to left* from foot of 1 in date. Upper left star very distant from L, almost as far as first star is from hair, between 2 and 3 mm.

REVERSE   *Only 12 arrows.* Point of star touches point of *upper part* of eagle's beak. Leaf point is under left side of stand of I in AMERICA. Die break from clouds under final S in STATES up through O to top of F and milling.   This is the most common variety of 1800 dollars.   Rarity 1.

1800.   B-17a

From same dies as B-17, but with additional die cracks as follows: Three cracks from lower left milling, one just under first star, two more parallel ones through curls into bust. Another break through 4th star, and a crack from 6th star to ribbon. Another crack between 11th and 12th stars. Reverse die break from AM to leaf. Rarity 2.

1800.   B-18 (H-18)

OBVERSE

From same die as B-13.

REVERSE

Now believed to be only a clashed die sub-variety of B-13.

Die break like a *spray* extending from tip of right eagle's wing through F and clouds to second and third stars on right.   Eagle's beak closed on point of star.   Leaf point is slightly right of center of I in AMERICA.   Letter A touches both 3rd and 4th feathers, and AM join at base.   Letters bifurcated.   Rarity 2.

1800.   B-18a

From same dies as B-18, but with two curved die breaks on obverse, one connecting first and fourth star, the other connecting 8th and 11th stars.   The reverse shows a fine die crack across shield and to right.   Rarity 3.

1800.   B-19 (H-19)

OBVERSE

Right stars close to Y and bust.   The last 0 in date is just as close to bust as last star.   The 1 almost touches curl.   Vertical *die flaw* below right side of first star near border.   The 7th star much farther from L than first star is from hair.   This specimen shows suction marks of the clouds about date, and of eagle's tail about E in LIBERTY.

REVERSE

From same die as B-11.   The AMERICAI variety.   Rarity 2.

1800. B-19a

From same dies as B-19, but with die crack along top of three upper left stars on obverse continuing along top of LIBE. Light suction marks above date. Rarity 3.

1800. B-19b

From same dies as B-19a, but with additional die crack on reverse along border above U, left top of N, down through I to left ribbon end. Suction marks around date and at sides. Rarity 3.

1800. B-20 (Obverse New)

OBVERSE   Obverse new, not known to Haseltine. The upper right star is in position *similar to the obverse of the 1804 dollars,* with two points almost touching Y. Therefore this variety has been used at least twice in idle fabrication of an 1804, by altering the last figure of date. The upper point of star nearly touches Y at a point *below* its top, as in the 1804 dollars. The 7th star is about as near L as last star is from bust. First star over 3 mm. from hair. As rare as an 1804.

REVERSE   From same die as B-4 and B-16. I have seen but a single specimen. Rarity 7

THE SILVER DOLLARS OF 1801, 1802, and 1803

THESE three dates have several things in common, relative to their coinage. The coinages were comparatively small during these years, of all varieties. Therefore, few reverse dies were made, since they could be used until worn out from use. Two reverse dies were used during all three years with various obverse dies. One of these reverse dies, reverse A, was used in no less than seven combinations or "marriages" to seven obverse dies during the three years. Another reverse, my reverse B, was also used in no less than seven marriages to as many obverse dies during the three years, 1801, 1802, and 1803. See plate.

The following is the limited coinage for these years:

1801   54,454 of all varieties
1802   41,650 of all varieties
1803   66,064 of all varieties

The die varieties are easily classified from the descriptions and plates.

Proof restrikes were coined of these three years at the same time that the 1804 dollars were first coined. They were all struck from the identical reverse die as used for the 1804, known as the "first reverse" of the 1804 dollar. The obverses for all of these issues were different from any other obverses. All of the proof restrikes of 1801, 1802, 1803, and 1804 are excessively rare, and probably about the same number coined of each. Reports vary from 6 to 12 pieces of each, and those of 1801, 1802, 1803 are just are rare as the 1804. The proof restrikes of 1801, 1802, and 1803 were in the old Mougey and Lyman collections. They appeared again in the sale of the "World's Greatest Collection" sold by the Numismatic Gallery in January 1945. None of these three rarities were in the Harlan P. Smith nor the Earle nor the Jenks sales. None were in the great Stickney collection, although there was the 1804 dollar.

1801. B-1 (H-1)

OBVERSE   Wide date, most space between 180, the 01 closest. The first 1 not very close to curl. The last 1 about as far from bust as first 1 is from curl. 8th star close to Y. Other three key stars are distant from L, hair, and bust. Small dot to left of center dot. Same dies as B-2 and B-3.

REVERSE   Point of star almost touches point of *lower part of eagle's beak*. 13 arrows. A in AMERICA touches 3rd and 4th feathers. Leaf point is under left side of upright of I in AMERICA. Rarity 4.

1801. B-2 (H-2)

OBVERSE   From same die as B-1 and B-3.   Suction marks around date.

REVERSE   The point of upper part of eagle's beak touches down on a point of a star slightly back from extreme star point.   Only 12 arrows show plainly (13th faintly shows, but is difficult to find).   First A in AMERICA touches third feather, and is connected by die break to 4th feather.   Leaf points more towards left corner of base of I in AMERICA.   Some specimens show a slight die break from cloud up through O to top of F.   Rarity 4.
See PLATE IX (Reverse A)   This same reverse was used for 1801 B-2; 1802 B-1, B-4, and B-6; 1803 B-4 and B-6.   The coinages were not large in any case.

1801. B-3 (H-3)

OBVERSE   From same die as B-1 and B-2.

REVERSE   Point of star *touches outside* of upper part of eagle's beak. *Right foot of all T's missing*.   A touches 3rd feather only. AME join at base.   Leaf *touches* I in AMERICA slightly right of center of base.   A slight crack from cloud up through OF differs from a similar crack in B-2.   Rarity 3.

1801. B-4 (H-4)

OBVERSE   Close date, figures evenly spaced.   The first 1 is very close to curl, the last 1 in date distant from bust.   The 8th star is about as near to Y as last star is from bust, slightly under 1 mm.   The 7th star is about 1½ mm. distant from L, and the first star about the same distance from curl.

REVERSE   There is a "spur" on the curved part of D.   Leaf points under center of I in AMERICA.   point of a star touches the outside of upper part of eagle's beak slightly above beak's point. Rarity 5.

[67]

See PLATE IX (Reverse B) This same die was used for 1801 B-4; 1802 B-2, B-3, B-5, and B-9; 1803 B-1 and B-5. The coinages were not large in any instance.

1801. B-5. Proof Restrike

OBVERSE The 8th star is distant from Y and the last star far from bust, about 2 mm. in each instance. A die crack passes along outside of two lowest stars on left through base of all figures of date to point of bust.

REVERSE *Struck from the identical die used for the famous 1804 dollars!* This is known as the "first reverse" on the 1804 dollar. Excessively rare. Rarity 8.

1802 over '01. B-1 (H-1)

OBVERSE "Pocket" at throat and "collar" at neck-line, at base. Close date, 02 closer than other figures. The 1 is very close to curl, but does not quite touch. The 8 centered between 1 and 0 but too low. A "dot" before upper lip under nose.

REVERSE See PLATE (Reverse A). This reverse was used in combination with no less than seven different obverse dies. Rarity 4.

1802 over '01. B-2 (H-2)

OBVERSE Wide date, the *most space* between 1 and 8. The 1 farther from curl than last. Last star close to bust. Uppermost wave centered under E.

REVERSE See PLATE (Reverse B). This reverse was used in combination with no less than six different obverse dies. Rarity 2.

1802 over '01. B-3 (H-3)

OBVERSE Wide overdate, with *most space* between 8 and 0.

REVERSE See PLATE (Reverse B). Rarity 3.

1802 over '01. B-4 (H-4)

OBVERSE Close date, the 1 *firmly touching curl.* The 8 is tipped slightly to right. Last star almost touches bust near junction of drapery with bosom. First star near hair, 8th near Y, and 7th distant from L. Base of B in LIBERTY is below base of E.

REVERSE   See PLATE (Reverse A). Rarity 5.

NOTE. See B-9 for newly discovered overdate.

1802.   B-5 (H-5)

OBVERSE   *Wide perfect date.* Figures of date *evenly spaced,* the 2 near bust.

REVERSE   See PLATE (Reverse B). Rarity 6.

1802.   B-6 (H-6)

OBVERSE   *Close perfect date. Wide space between 8 and 0.* The figure 2 is distant from bust. Right foot of T in LIBERTY missing.

REVERSE   See PLATE (Reverse A). Rarity 1.

NOTE. There is no number 7. The coin described by Haseltine as H-6 is the identical coin described in the "addenda" as No. 7. It is described as "Obverse same as No. 6; reverse same as No. 4". That *is* number 6, since number 4 and 6 have the identical reverse.

1802.   B-8.   Proof Restrike

OBVERSE   The 2 in date is *curled* at top, differing from any other obverse. The last two stars are joined at inner points. The 7th star is distant from the L, more distant than first star is from hair.

REVERSE   Struck from the identical die used for the famous 1804 dollars. This is known as the "first reverse" of the 1804 dollar. Excessively rare. Rarity 8.

1802 over '01.   B-9.   (Obverse new)

OBVERSE   The figures of date are small and well spaced, the 8 centered between 1 and 0 and not too low as in No. 1, nor tipped to right, as in No. 4. Look at the overdate 2 over 1, and observe that the left top of 1 under 2 is in line with left top and base of 2. A flaw in the die shows midway between base of B in LIBERTY and end of curl on head just beneath. Liberty has closed lips, while the mouth is open on all other overdates.

REVERSE See PLATE IX (Reverse B). Rarity 8.
NOTE. The above coin was discovered by Mr. Bolender after the plates for this book were completed. It was unexpectedly found in a general collection that was purchased in the course of his business. It is the only piece known to him.

1803. B-1 (H-1)

OBVERSE Thin top to 3 in date, right top of 3 slanting toward bust, short left tip slanting toward 0. Stars equi-distant from Y and bust, and close. The 8th star is in same relative position to Y as on the 1804 dollar. Liberty's mouth open. Letters much bifurcated. Light die crack from milling through left side of R to hair.

REVERSE See PLATE (Reverse B). This die has been combined with no less than seven different obverses. Rarity 5.

1803. B-2 (H-2)

OBVERSE Thin top to 3, top parallel to bust, left tip parallel to 0. The 3 is lower than other figures, and the 1 defective at top. Upper stars equi-distant from L and Y. First star distant from hair.

Now believed that no such variety exists.

REVERSE 12 arrows show plainly, and 13th faint. See PLATE (Reverse A). Rarity 6.

1803. B-3 (H-3)

OBVERSE Thin top to 3, position of 3 similar to B-1, but 8th star is more distant from Y. Close date.

REVERSE AM touch at base. Point of star *touches* point of *lower part* of eagle's beak. Very short stem in claw. Rarity 6.

1803. B-4 (H-4)

OBVERSE Thin top to 3, top side long, and ends near bust, very close. 1 firmly touches curl. Last star almost touches bust, first star near hair. Upper stars distant from L and Y.

REVERSE   See PLATE (Reverse A).   Rarity 3.

1803.   B-5 (H-5)

OBVERSE   Thin 3 to top, the 3 too high.   Figures of date all close.   8th and 13th stars about equi-distant Y and bust, and much closer than first and 7th stars are from hair and L.   The 3 almost touches bust, and 1 is near curl.

REVERSE   See PLATE (Reverse B).   Rarity 5.

1803.   B-5a

From same dies as B-5, but the letters are bifurcated.   Rarity 5.

1803.   B-6 (H-6)

OBVERSE   Thick top to 3 in date.   Last star close to bust.   First star distant from hair, about $2\frac{1}{3}$ mm.   The 180 wide, and 3 a trifle low at base.

REVERSE   See PLATE (Reverse A).   Rarity 2.

1803.   B-6a

From same dies as B-6, but with a fine die crack connecting all stars on right.   Rarity 4.

1803.   B-7.   Proof Restrike

OBVERSE   Thick 3.   Stars on left distant, the 7th farther from L than first star is from hair.   Highest curl on top of head about centered under upright of E, and next top curl centered under R.

REVERSE   *Struck from the identical die used for the famous 1804 dollars!* This is known as the "first reverse" of the 1804 dollar.   See plate.   Excessively rare.   Rarity 8.

THE 1804 DOLLARS

THE few rare and famous silver dollars of 1804 are so well-known to collectors, that it was the intention of the author to omit this paragraph. The purpose of this book has been to untangle what was formerly regarded as a difficult task, the correct attribution of the silver dollars from 1794 to 1803. So many interesting articles have been written about the 1804 dollars, that the author has nothing new to add. However, since they are of the same general type as the other early dollars of the years just preceding, we add this paragraph.

It is the opinion of the author, and generally regarded as correct, that all 1804 dollars are restrikes, that is, struck some years after the year 1804. The 1804 dollar was first known about 1843 when Matthew Stickney secured a specimen from the Philadelphia mint in exchange for coins from his collection that the mint collection lacked. Of this "first variety" only six specimens are known. The reverse die shows a die crack through the top of NITED of UNITED extending to top of left wing. The second T in STATES is a little to the right of being over the center of the cloud. This same reverse die was used for the restrikes of 1801 B-5, 1802 B-8, and 1803 B-7.

The same obverse die was used with another reverse die for a "second variety" struck some years later but before 1878. The reverse die shows the second T in STATES more over the left portion of the cloud, and the E in STATES above the space between two clouds. Of this variety about seven specimens are known.

The mint records show silver dollar coinage in 1804, but in all probability those dollars actually coined in 1804 were all dated 1803, and the dated 1804 dollars were struck some years later.

Bibliography—For the best suppplementary reading on our early silver dollars, write to the American Numismatic Society, Broadway at 156th St., New York, N.Y. for Numismatic Notes and Monographs No. 95, by Arthur D. McIlvaine, *The Silver Dollars of the United States of America*, 1941. 36 pp. 1 folded plate, price $1.00. There is very little repetition in these works, and 10 pages are devoted to the 1804 dollar.

Interested persons should inqure of the A.N.S. concerning the continued availability of the above-mentioned booklet and/or its current price.

Further recommended reading on the 1804 silver dollars is the definitive study *The Fantastic 1804 Dollar* by Eric P. Newman and Kenneth E. Bressett. Published in 1962 by Whitman, it is still available from several of the leading dealers in numismatic books.

It is now known that the 1804-dated silver dollars were first struck in 1834, at the order of Mint Director Samuel Moore, for inclusion in special presentation proof sets of U.S. coins destined for the Imam of Oman and the King of Siam.

The author's statement on the facing page that only six specimens of the "first variety" 1804 dollar are known is incorrect. There are, in fact, two more such coins, struck during the 1830s and 1840s.

Of the second variety, the author is correct in numbering them at seven specimens These were struck in the late 1850s and early 1860s to provide specimens for well-connected coin collectors of the day and to allow the Mint to trade examples of the already-famous coin for material to complete its own coin cabinet.

Known specimens of the 1804 silver dollar are enumerated here:

FIRST VARIETY

1) Smithsonian Institution specimen; from the U.S. Mint cabinet.

2) Louis Eliasberg specimen; obtained by Matthew A. Stickney from the Mint Cabinet in 1843, then through the collections of Col. James W. Ellsworth, Wayte Raymond, and William Cutler Atwater.

3) Specimen in the 1834 proof set currently owned by David Spink, of Spink & Son, London. As of mid-1980, the set was being offered in the numismatic market at $1 million. Belived to be the set presented to the King of Siam on April 5, 1836.

4) C.F. Childs Collection specimen. Believed to be the coin from the proof set presented to the Imam of Oman and from which it passed through the collections of C.A. Watters, Virgil Brand and Charles E. Green.

5) Harold Bareford Collection specimen; traced back to the Adolph Weyl auction of 1884, to the Chapman Bros. personal holdings and through the collections of James B. Dexter, H.G. Brown, Willam F. Dunham, and Charles M. Williams.

6) Byron Reed Collection specimen now owned by the city of Omaha, Neb. Purchased by E.H. Sanford around 1868, sold in 1874 and later part of the Lorin G. Parmalee Collection.

7) Massachusetts Historical Society specimen sold in 1970. Earlier the property of pioneer numismatist Joseph J. Mickley who it is believed obtained it from a Philadelphia bank teller who acquired it at face value as part of a deposit. Then through the collections of W.A. Lilliendahl and William S. Appleton.

8) Willis DuPont specimen, stolen in 1967. Earlier from the collections of Col. Mendes I. Cohen, Henry S. Adams, Lorin G. Parmalee, H.G. Sampson, William B. Wetmore, Elmer Sears and Lammont DuPont.

SECOND VARIETY

9) Mint Cabinet specimen, unique variety with plain edge, struck over a Swiss shooting taler, circa 1859.

10) Garrett Collection specimen sold March 26, 1980, for $400,000 to Larry Hanks. Subsequently re-sold for undisclosed price. Possibly acquired from the Mint by William Idler, it may also have come from Koch & Co., Vienna, Austria, to the collection of O.H. Berg, Baltimore, from which it was purchased for $765 by T. Harrison Garrett in 1883.

11) Amon Carter specimen; from the collections of John Haseltine, Phineas Adams, Henry Ahlborn, Lyman H. Low, Waldo Newcomer, Col. E.H.R. Green, A.J. Allen, and F.C.C. Boyd.

12) Louis Wolfson specimen; through the hands of John W. Haseltine (1877), R. Coulton Davis & John Hale (1890), R.H. Mull (1950), "Fairbanks Collection," (1960).

13) Willis DuPont specimen; from the collection of Philadelphia Mint Director H.R. Linderman to the James Ten Eyck Collection to DuPont.

14) American Numismatic Society specimen; donated by The Chase Manhattan Bank Money Museum and earlier owned by Farran Zerbe. Earlier the property of the Guttag Bros., Wayte Raymond, Col. James W. Ellsworth, Isaac Rosenthal, and possibly W. Julius Driefus.

15) Jerry Buss Collection specimen; possibly the best known of the 1804 dollars. Originated with William Idler, it went to the H.O. Granberg Collection to William Cutler Atwater in 1946, then through the hands of the following collectors and dealers, Will W. Neil, Edwin Hydeman, World Wide Coin Co., Bowers and Ruddy Galleries, Continental Coin Co., an unnamed Swiss Bank and Superior Galleries. Sold by Bowers and Ruddy in 1974 for $225,000; Buss was able to obtain the coin for a reported $200,000.

Plate I

1794

1
1

1-10-16
2-17-19
3-9-11
4

5
6-a
7-18-20
8

12
6-13
14
15

1-2-13
3
1795
4-9
5-6-12

Plate II

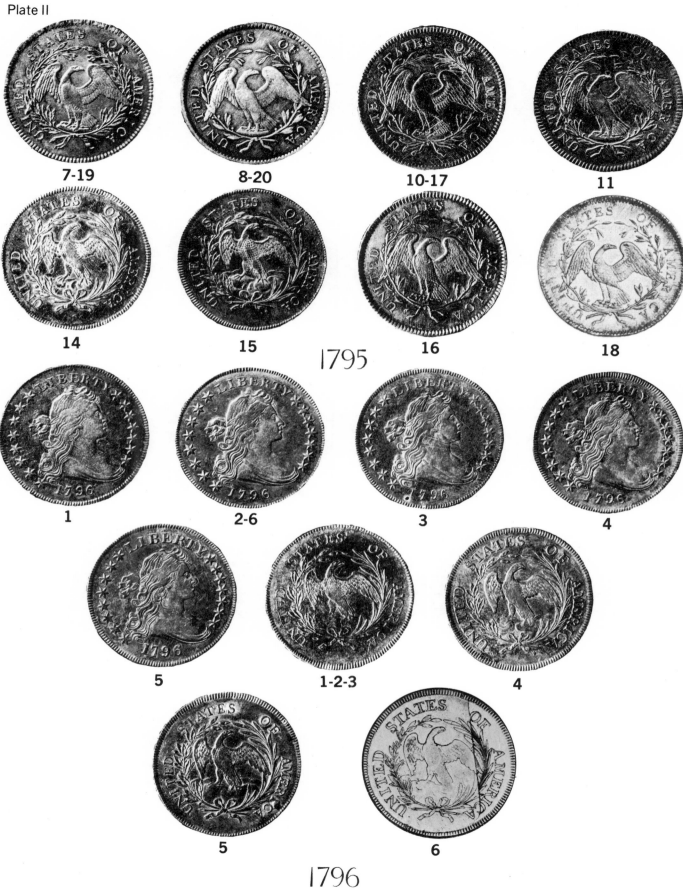

7-19   8-20   10-17   11

14   15   16   18

1795

1   2-6   3   4

5   1-2-3   4

5   6

1796

Plate III

1-2

3

1

2

3

1797

1-32

2

3-4-5

6-7

8

9

10-13

11

1798

Plate IV

12

14

15

16

17

19

18-20-21

22-23

24

25

25b

26

27

28-30-31-33

29

1

2

3-7-20

4-32

5

1798

Plate V

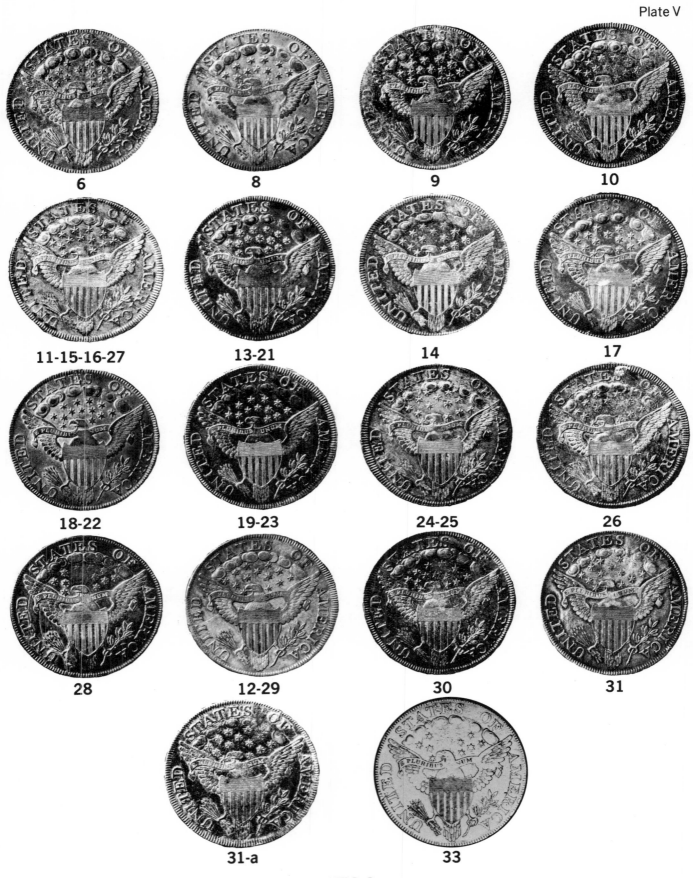

6

8

9

10

11-15-16-27

13-21

14

17

18-22

19-23

24-25

26

28

12-29

30

31

31-a

33

1798

Plate VI

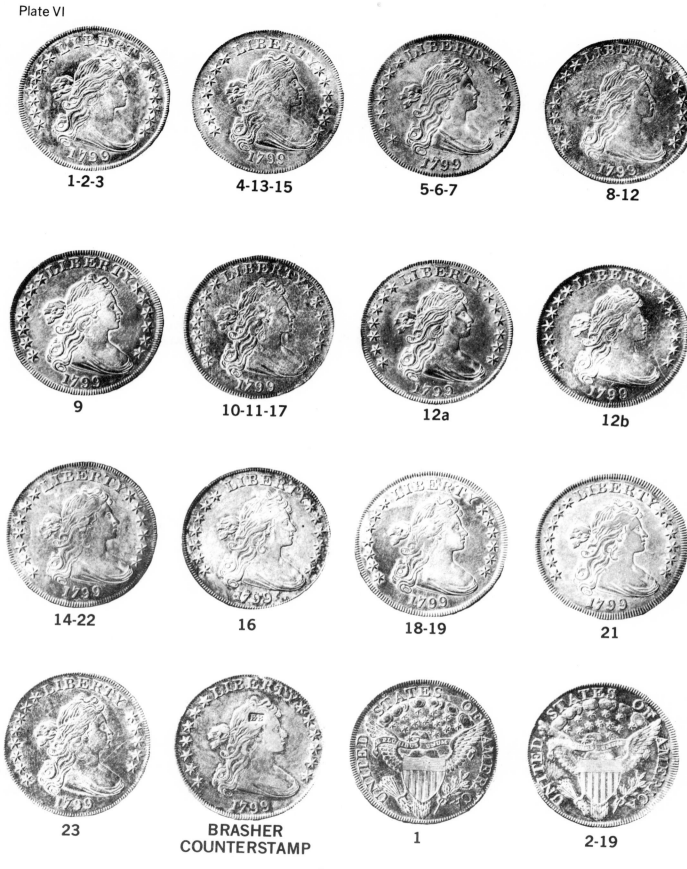

1-2-3

4-13-15

5-6-7

8-12

9

10-11-17

12a

12b

14-22

16

18-19

21

23

**BRASHER
COUNTERSTAMP**

1

2-19

1799

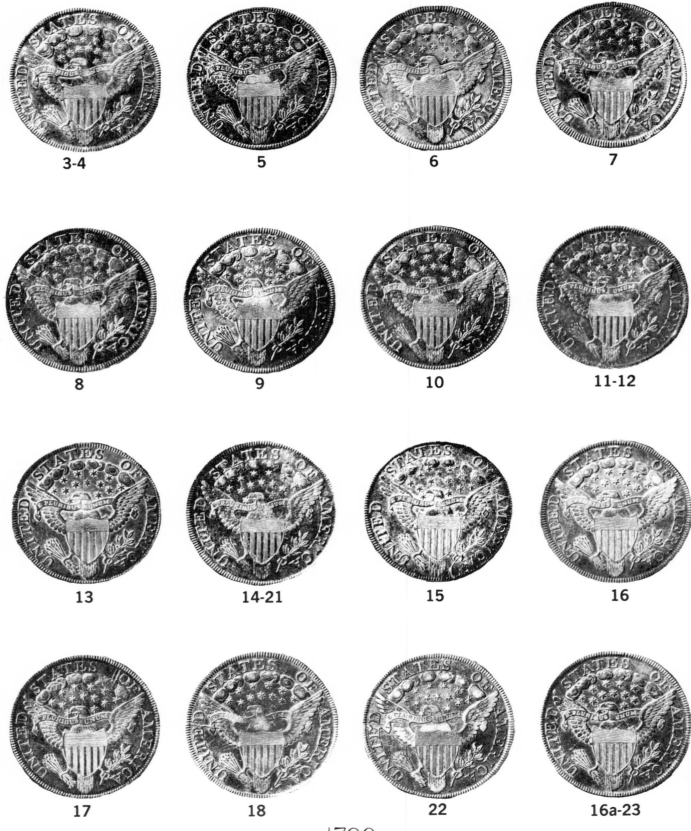

Plate VII

3-4

5

6

7

8

9

10

11-12

13

14-21

15

16

17

18

22

16a-23

1799

Plate VIII

1

4

4a

5-8

10-11

2-3-12

14

15

16

13-18

17

19

20

1-2

3

5-10

8

11-19

12

14

15

4-16-20

1800

17

18

Plate IX

1801 - 1802 - 1803

Early U.S. Silver Dollar Grading Guide

Excerpted from

"The Official American Numismatic Association
Grading Standards for United States Coins"
through the courtesy of the
American Numismatic Association.

DOLLARS—FLOWING HAIR 1794–1795

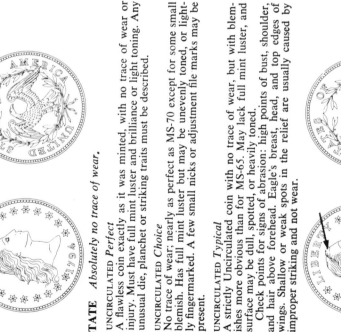

MINT STATE *Absolutely no trace of wear.*

MS-70 UNCIRCULATED *Perfect*
A flawless coin exactly as it was minted, with no trace of wear or injury. Must have full mint luster and brilliance or light toning. Any unusual die, planchet or striking traits must be described.

MS-65 UNCIRCULATED *Choice*
No trace of wear; nearly as perfect as MS-70 except for some small blemish. Has full mint luster but may be unevenly toned, or lightly fingermarked. A few small nicks or adjustment file marks may be present.

MS-60 UNCIRCULATED *Typical*
A strictly Uncirculated coin with no trace of wear, but with blemishes more obvious than for MS-65. May lack full mint luster, and surface may be dull, spotted, or heavily toned.

Check points for signs of abrasion: high points of bust, shoulder, and hair above forehead. Eagle's breast, head, and top edges of wings. Shallow or weak spots in the relief are usually caused by improper striking and not wear.

ABOUT UNCIRCULATED *Small trace of wear visible on highest points.*

AU-55 *Choice*
OBVERSE: Only a trace of wear shows on highest points of hair above forehead.
REVERSE: A trace of wear shows on breast.
Three-quarters of the mint luster is still present.

AU-50 *Typical*
OBVERSE: Traces of wear show on hair above and beside forehead.
REVERSE: Traces of wear show on breast and head.
Half of the mint luster is still present.

DOLLARS—FLOWING HAIR 1794-1795

EXTREMELY FINE *Very light wear on only the highest points.*

EF-45 *Choice*
OBVERSE: Slight wear shows on high points of hair from forehead to neck. Very light wear at eyebrow, shoulder and bust line. Stars fully detailed.
REVERSE: High points of wings, breast and head are lightly worn. Lines in feathers are clearly defined.
Part of the mint luster is still present.

EF-40 *Typical*
OBVERSE: Wear shows on hair from forehead to neck, and lightly on the cheek and bust. Lightly worn at neck line in spots. Stars fully detailed.
REVERSE: High points of eagle are worn, but each detail is clearly defined. Head, wings and breast are lightly worn.
Traces of mint luster can be seen.

VERY FINE *Light to moderate even wear. All major features are sharp.*

VF-30 *Choice*
OBVERSE: Three-quarters of flowing hair details show. Hair above forehead is worn but has some bold features. Parts of star centers, eyebrow and ear are very weak.
REVERSE: Feathers are worn but more than half of the wing details are visible. Some of the details in head and breast are clear unless weakly struck.

VF-20 *Typical*
OBVERSE: Half of the details still show in hair. Eyebrow, ear and bust are worn but bold. Parts of shoulder are smooth. Every letter and star is plainly visible. Star centers are nearly flat.
REVERSE: Head and breast are worn, but some feathers are visible. Half of details in wings and tail are clear.

DOLLARS—FLOWING HAIR 1794-1795

FINE *Moderate to heavy even wear. Entire design clear and bold.*

F-12
OBVERSE: Some details show in hair ends, and below ear. All letters, date and stars are visible. The ear and eye are clear. Hair at top of forehead is outlined.
REVERSE: Some feathers are visible in body, wings and tail. Breast and head are smooth. Eye is visible. Letters in legend are worn but clear.

VERY GOOD *Well worn. Design clear but flat and lacking details.*

VG-8
OBVERSE: Entire head is weak, and most hair details are worn smooth. Date and LIBERTY are weak but clear. Parts of the eye and ear are visible. Stars are outlined.
REVERSE: Eagle is boldly outlined with only a few details showing in wings and tail. Breast is smooth. Some letters are very weak.

GOOD *Heavily worn. Design and legend visible but faint in spots.*

G-4
OBVERSE: Entire design worn smooth with very little detail remaining. Legend, stars and date are well worn but all visible.
REVERSE: Eagle worn flat but is completely outlined. Tops of some letters are worn nearly smooth.

DOLLARS—FLOWING HAIR 1794–1795

ABOUT GOOD *Outlined design. Parts of date and legend worn smooth.*

AG-3 OBVERSE: Head is outlined with nearly all details worn away. Date readable but very weak. Stars merging into rim.
REVERSE: Entire design flat and partially worn away.

Note: Examples of this design are often weakly struck, particularly on the eagle's breast and feathers. File adjustment marks are frequently seen, and are a normal part of the manufacturing process.

1794 is usually weakly struck at date, UNITED, and stars on left side of obverse.

DOLLARS—DRAPED BUST, SMALL EAGLE 1795–1798

MINT STATE *Absolutely no trace of wear.*

MS-70 UNCIRCULATED *Perfect*
A flawless coin exactly as it was minted, with no trace of wear or injury. Must have full mint luster and brilliance or light toning. Any unusual die or striking traits must be described.

MS-65 UNCIRCULATED *Choice*
No trace of wear; nearly as perfect as MS-70 except for some small blemish. Has full mint luster but may be unevenly toned, or lightly fingermarked. A few small nicks or adjustment file marks may be present.

MS-60 UNCIRCULATED *Typical*
A strictly Uncirculated coin with no trace of wear, but with blemishes more obvious than for MS-65. May lack full mint luster, and surface may be dull, spotted, or heavily toned.
Check points for signs of abrasion: high points of bust, shoulder, and hair above forehead. Eagle's breast and top edges of wings. Shallow or weak spots in the relief are usually caused by improper striking and not wear.

ABOUT UNCIRCULATED *Small trace of wear visible on highest points.*

AU-55 *Choice*
OBVERSE: Only a trace of wear shows on highest points of hair above forehead.
REVERSE: A trace of wear shows on breast.
Three-quarters of the mint luster is still present.

AU-50 *Typical*
OBVERSE: Trace of wear shows on hair above and beside forehead. Drapery has trace of wear at shoulder and bust line.
REVERSE: Traces of wear show on breast and left leg.
Half of the mint luster is still present.

DOLLARS—DRAPED BUST, SMALL EAGLE 1795–1798

EXTREMELY FINE *Very light wear on only the highest points.*

EF-45 *Choice*
OBVERSE: Slight wear shows on high points of hair from forehead to the ear. Drapery is worn at shoulder and bust line.
REVERSE: High points of wing tips, breast and left leg are lightly worn. Lines in feathers are clearly defined.
Part of the mint luster is still present.

EF-40 *Typical*
OBVERSE: Wear shows on hair from forehead to ear, and lightly on the cheek and bust. Drapery lightly worn at neck line in spots.
REVERSE: High points of wings are worn, but each detail is clearly defined. Left leg and breast are slightly worn.
Traces of mint luster can be seen.

VERY FINE *Light to moderate even wear. All major features are sharp.*

VF-30 *Choice*
OBVERSE: Three-quarters of hair details show. Hair above forehead is worn but has some bold features. Parts of drapery are worn smooth.
REVERSE: Wing edges are worn but most central details are visible. Some of the details in left leg and breast are clear unless weakly struck.

VF-20 *Typical*
OBVERSE: Over half of the details still show in hair. Forehead and bust are worn but bold. Parts of drapery are smooth. Letters and star centers are plainly visible.
REVERSE: Left leg and breast are worn, but some feathers are visible. About three-quarters of details in wings are clear.

DOLLARS—DRAPED BUST, SMALL EAGLE 1795–1798

FINE *Moderate to heavy even wear. Entire design clear and bold.*

F-12
OBVERSE: Some details show in hair ends, curls and at left of ear. All letters, date and stars are visible. The eye and ear are clear. Bust is worn with few drapery lines remaining.
REVERSE: Half the feathers are visible in wings. Breast and left leg are smooth. Letters in legend are worn but clear.

VERY GOOD *Well worn. Design clear but flat and lacking details.*

VG-8
OBVERSE: Entire head is weak, and most hair details and drapery are worn smooth. Date and LIBERTY are weak but clear. Parts of the eye and ear are visible. Stars are outlined.
REVERSE: Eagle is boldly outlined with only a few details showing in wings. Breast and left leg are smooth. Some letters are very weak. Rim is full.

GOOD *Heavily worn. Design and legend visible but faint in spots.*

G-4
OBVERSE: Entire design work smooth with very little detail remaining. Legend, stars and date are well worn but visible.
REVERSE: Eagle is worn flat and only outlined. Tops of some letters are worn nearly smooth. Rim is full.

DOLLARS—DRAPED BUST, HERALDIC EAGLE
1798–1804

MINT STATE *Absolutely no trace of wear.*

MS-70 UNCIRCULATED *Perfect*
A flawless coin exactly as it was minted, with no trace of wear or injury. Must have full mint luster and brilliance or light toning. Any unusual die or striking traits must be described.

MS-65 UNCIRCULATED *Choice*
No trace of wear; nearly as perfect as MS-70 except for some small blemish. Has full mint luster but may be unevenly toned, or lightly fingermarked. A few small nicks or adjustment file marks may be present.

MS-60 UNCIRCULATED *Typical*
A strictly Uncirculated coin with no trace of wear, but with blemishes more obvious than for MS-65. May lack full mint luster, and surface may be dull, spotted, or heavily toned.
Check points for signs of abrasion: high points of bust, shoulder, and hair above forehead. Eagle's head, breast, edges of wings, and clouds. Shallow or weak spots in the motto are usually caused by improper striking and not wear.

ABOUT UNCIRCULATED *Small trace of wear visible on highest points.*

AU-55 *Choice*
OBVERSE: Only a trace of wear shows on highest points of hair above forehead.
REVERSE: A trace of wear shows on the clouds.
Three-quarters of the mint luster is still present.

AU-50 *Typical*
OBVERSE: Trace of wear shows on hair above and behind forehead. Drapery has trace of wear at shoulder and bust line.
REVERSE: Traces of wear show on breast feathers and clouds.
Half of the mint luster is still present.

DOLLARS—DRAPED BUST, SMALL EAGLE 1795–1798

ABOUT GOOD *Outlined design. Parts of date and legend worn smooth.*

AG-3 OBVERSE: Head is outlined with nearly all details worn away. Date readable but very weak. Stars merging into rim.
REVERSE: Entire design flat and partially worn away. Legend merges with rim.

Note: Examples of this design are often weakly struck, particularly on the eagle's breast and feathers. File adjustment marks are occasionally seen, and are a normal part of the manufacturing process.

1796, small date and letters. The reverse is usually weak.
1797, 7 stars right, small letters. The reverse is always weak.
1798, 15 stars. The reverse is usually weak.

DOLLARS—DRAPED BUST, HERALDIC EAGLE
1798–1804

FINE *Moderate to heavy even wear. Entire design clear and bold.*

F-12 OBVERSE: Some details show in hair ends, curls and at left of ear. All letters, date and stars are visible. The eye and ear are clear. Bust is worn with few drapery lines remaining.

REVERSE: Half the feathers are visible in wings. Breast and head are smooth. Letters in legend are worn but clear. Clouds and top of shield show considerable wear.

VERY GOOD *Well worn. Design clear but flat and lacking details.*

VG-8 OBVERSE: Entire head is weak, and most hair details and drapery are worn smooth. Date and LIBERTY are weak but clear. Parts of the eye and ear are visible. Stars are outlined with some tips worn flat.

REVERSE: Eagle is boldly outlined with only a few details showing in wings. Clouds, head and top of shield are smooth. Some letters in legend are very weak; parts of motto are missing. Rim is full.

GOOD *Heavily worn. Design and legend visible but faint in spots.*

DOLLARS—DRAPED BUST, HERALDIC EAGLE
1798–1804

EXTREMELY FINE *Very light wear on only the highest points.*

EF-45 *Choice*

OBVERSE: Slight wear shows on high points of hair from forehead to the ear. Drapery is worn at shoulder and bust line.

REVERSE: High points of wing edges, breast feathers, and clouds are lightly worn. Lines in shield are clearly defined.

Part of the mint luster is still present.

EF-40 *Typical*

OBVERSE: Wear shows on hair from forehead to ear, and lightly on the cheek and bust. Drapery lightly worn at neck line in spots.

REVERSE: High points of clouds and wings are worn, but each detail is clearly defined. Head and breast are slightly worn. Lines in shield are separated.

Traces of mint luster can be seen.

VERY FINE *Light to moderate even wear. All major features are sharp.*

VF-30 *Choice*

OBVERSE: Three-quarters of hair details show. Hair at back of head is worn but has some bold features. Parts of drapery are worn smooth.

REVERSE: Wing edges are worn but three-quarters of central details are visible. Clouds, head and motto show wear.

Horizontal shield lines worn but separated.

VF-20 *Typical*

OBVERSE: Over half of the details still show in hair. Forehead and bust are worn but bold. Parts of drapery are smooth. Letters and star centers are plainly visible.

REVERSE: Head and breast are worn, but some feathers are visible. Some lines in shield are merged together. About three-quarters of details in wings are clear. Motto is complete.

DOLLARS—DRAPED BUST, HERALDIC EAGLE
1798–1804

G-4   OBVERSE: Entire design worn smooth with very little detail remaining. Legend, stars and date are well worn but visible.

REVERSE: Eagle is worn flat and only outlined. Tops of some letters are worn nearly smooth. Only half of the stars are completely outlined. Rim is full.

ABOUT GOOD   *Outlined design. Parts of date and legend worn smooth.*

AG-3   OBVERSE: Head is outlined with nearly all details worn away. Date readable but very weak. Stars merging into rim.

REVERSE: Entire design flat and partially worn away. Legend merges with rim.

Note: Examples of this design are often weakly struck, particularly on the motto, shield, clouds and wing feathers. File adjustment marks are occasionally seen, and are a normal part of the manufacturing process.

NOTES

NOTES

NOTES